5/22/91

To Rose Ann

Thank You

For Your

Continuous

Support

Art Murett

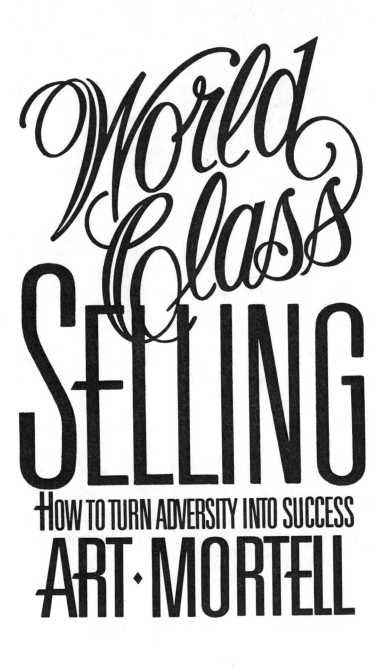

World Class SELLING

How to Turn Adversity into Success

ART · MORTELL

Dearborn
Financial Publishing, Inc.

While a great deal of care has been taken to provide accurate and current information, the ideas, suggestions, general principles and conclusions presented in this book
are subject to local, state and federal laws and regulations, court cases and any revi-
sions of same. The reader is thus urged to consult legal counsel regarding any points
of law—this publication should not be used as a substitute for competent legal advice.

Publisher: Kathleen A. Welton
Associate Editor: Karen A. Christensen
Senior Project Editor: Jack L. Kiburz

©1991 by Art Mortell

Published by Dearborn Financial Publishing, Inc.

Printed in the United States of America

91 92 93 10 9 8 7 6 5 4 3 2 1

Library of Congress Cataloging-in-Publication Data

Mortell, Art.
    World class selling : how to turn adversity into success / Art Mortell.
        p.   cm.
    Includes index.
    ISBN 0-7931-0275-8
    1. Selling.   2. Success in business.   I. Title.
HF5438.25.M675   1991
658.8′5 — dc20   91-8925
                                                                           CIP

Table of Contents

Introduction

We are living in the third transformation. For the first time in history, we are becoming one society—global; one economy—free enterprise; and one politics—free democracy. Think of the effect this will have on us as salespeople.

Consider the qualities required to succeed in this global society. We need to be able to communicate, express ideas, make effective presentations, develop relationships, deal with confrontation, manage ourselves, be persuasive, sell people on our ideas, gain results, manage stress and be self-disciplined.

Historically, there have been only three life-styles. In the beginning, we were nomadic; we were hunters and gatherers. We had no time to think, except to ensure survival. We had no permanent home; we kept moving, following the animal herds and the changing of the seasons. We carried our home or found a cave for the night. We were migratory.

Then came the first transformation. We left the nomadic life-style and became agricultural. With domesticated animals, we had no need to hunt, and, hopefully, we had a good harvest and the grainery was full. Now we had time to think. We became great philosophers, artists and architects. Most people never traveled more than ten miles beyond their place of birth. We built cities, temples and pyramids.

Next came the second transformation, from an agricultural to an industrial life-style. We left the farms to work in the factories. Our work became routine and structured. We followed instructions. We sat in the same places and spoke only when spoken to.

The third transformation was symbolized by the events of 1989, which may have been the greatest year in the history of the world. What took ten years to occur in Poland took only one year to ten days to occur in Czechoslovakia and Hungary. It happened in one night at the Berlin Wall. The government of the Soviet Union finally recognized that, as noble as its thesis of no homeless or unemployed might be, the most productive and economically competitive society is one which is market-driven.

This brings us to the question: What qualities will be required to succeed as a salesperson in a market-driven economy?

What is the single human attribute which causes us to be competitively successful? Some people claim the key factor is our dexterity, such as using our hands to operate machines and technology. Of course, those people who are good with their hands, such as machinists and carpenters, make good incomes.

We also know that the ability to communicate and express ideas is increasingly important. Movie stars and politicians, who are persuasive and project charismatic images, often create magnetic reactions which result in financial success and popularity. Ronald Reagan, referred to as the Great Communicator, was one of the most popular presidents in the history of the United States.

Even more so, a key factor for success is intelligence, our ability to reason and solve problems. Those people in our society who are particularly intelligent, such as scientists and professors, gain money and positions of prestige.

There is, however, a quality that is more important than intelligence or the ability to reason and be creative. This attribute takes us competitively beyond the animals and even other people. It is being *risk-oriented.*

Consider two parts of your personality. First, you are competent, rational and intelligent. Second, you are courageous, adventuresome and risk-oriented. There will be days in the future, however, when you reach a crossroads in which you can be introspective or take chances, but not both at the same time. In the long run, success is based not on being creative and brilliant but on confronting risk and taking chances. In other words, extending ourselves and staying adventuresome, as with Columbus, even though fearful of "falling off the edge," are the qualities that epitomize the successful world-class salesperson.

While lecturing internationally since 1967, I have found that people want to go beyond the basics of selling and understand how to

- Stay motivated, even when experiencing adversity;
- Persevere, regardless of confronting hostility;
- Become stimulated by stress;
- Move prospects effortlessly toward agreement;
- Develop the unique kind of relationships which culminate in the desired results;
- Turn the prospect's resistance into receptivity;
- Gain the buying decision through advanced concepts and techniques;
- Cause almost everyone to feel comfortable with you;
- Eliminate negative feelings and develop your potential; and
- Enhance your self-image, even when in conflict and frustrated.

World Class Selling was written to excite, motivate, entertain and enlighten you to extend yourself beyond familiar boundaries. My objective is to show you how to understand yourself better and thereby improve both your relationships and your results. In the process, you will learn how to better manage resistance. I dedicate this book to you. Renew your adventuresome spirit by setting high expectations and, regardless of what happens, enjoy the trip!

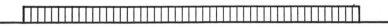

PART

1

How To Enjoy Failure, Be Amused by Rejection and Thrive on Anxiety

1

Enjoying Failure

People are remembered in life, not for how few times they fail, but for how often they succeed.

Consider three questions:

- Have you ever encountered failure?
- Have you ever been rejected and taken it personally?
- Have you ever experienced anxiety?

Now think of how you can enjoy failure, be amused by rejection and thrive on anxiety.

Three types of people try to succeed in selling. First are those who take failure and rejection too much to heart and, under considerable stress, soon resign. Many businesses often lose 20 to 60 percent of their salespeople during the first year. Next are people who demand to excel. They have high expectations, persevere and eventually achieve their objectives. They also, however, take failure and rejection too personally and, while becoming financially successful, too often experience such accompanying ailments as hypertension, drug addiction and alcoholism.

The third person is the one with whom you may want to identify. These people also demand to excel, for they have high expectations. However, they have developed unique reactions to failure, rejection and anxiety without which such experiences each day they become irritable and restless.

Consider where you are within this spectrum in Figure 1.1.

Figure 1.1   Success Spectrum

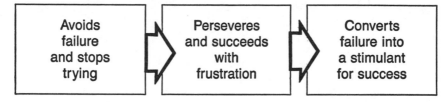

| Avoids failure and stops trying | Perseveres and succeeds with frustration | Converts failure into a stimulant for success |

ANTICIPATION

Before we discuss why successful people thrive on adversity, consider an experience which can be more dangerous than failure. Often more immobilizing than failure itself is the fear, the thought or anticipation of failure. The opposite also is true: More exhilarating than success itself is often the anticipation of succeeding. Equally immobilizing of our enthusiasm is not the experience of defeat, but the fear, the thought or the anticipation of failing.

For example, there was a newspaper article about a man skydiving. He pulled the cord and the chute did not open, and in panic he never pulled the emergency cord. As a self-fulfilling prophecy, fear can cause us to do what we are fearful will happen. In other words, the sky diver panicked and was unable to function properly.

Fear can immobilize us.

More recently, there was another article about a man skydiving. He pulled the cord and the chute did not open. He pulled the emergency cord, which also did not open. At 3,000 feet, he thought to himself, 'What the hell,' or words to that effect.

Now those who are experienced sky divers will tell you that if you are in trouble to land on the front of your feet and then go into an immediate tumble or acrobatic roll in which there is no direct impact on the land. When the sky diver landed after falling from 3,000 feet, his ankles broke instantly, yet no other bones were broken. His entire body suffered abrasions, bruising and bleeding, but not one more broken bone. He had gone into a continuous acrobatic roll. The man who could have survived died and the man to whom you would not have given odds survived. We are discussing not only the challenge of dealing with adversity, but also how to deal with the thought, fear or anticipation of defeat.

Imagine the day is hot and the pool of water is so inviting. You touch the water and it is cold. Now the thought of being in the pool turns you off. Yet if you jumped in, though the first moments might be as cold as you anticipated, you soon are stimulated and refreshed.

Selling is the same. You are excited about succeeding. Yet the more you think of prospecting, the more you are turned off. You pick up the telephone and it is "heavy" in your hand. If, however, you were to make the first call, and even the prospect were cold toward you, you are in motion. After a few more calls, you may score a positive response and now are stimulated and in positive momentum.

As a last prefacing thought, you cannot fail. Failure actually does not exist. *All that exists are experiences that are less than what you expected from which you must demand: "What have I gained? What was the benefit?"* Think of the benefits from those experiences which were less than what you expected.

EXPECTATIONS, PERCEPTIONS AND REACTIONS

Failure and success are synonymous.

They are only experiences. The difference between failure and success can be expressed in three words: *expectations, perceptions* and *reactions*. Whatever happens in your life, whether winning or losing, being loved or rejected, experiencing elation or depression, neither is a result of luck or astrology. Rather, your results are by-products of your reactions, which are dictated by your perceptions of reality and originate from your expectations.

One child gets a B and another child, a C. Who is elated and who is depressed? The child with the B is depressed, for he or she expected an A. The child with the C is elated, for he or she expected either a D or to fail. What you take from the experience is what makes you more aware of how good you are.

In the same context, consider a salesperson who makes 12 cold calls, gets 12 nos in a row and quits for the rest of the day. He or she may use direct mail, read the *Wall Street Journal* or call friends to discuss the weekend's social gathering, but will avoid any further confrontation or risk of defeat. Another salesperson, however, may need

30 nos in a row in the morning just to wake up and feel good. From where do these reactions originate? They originate from our perceptions of reality as dictated by our expectations.

Reactions Influence Feelings

Our reactions trigger our *feelings*. Have you ever experienced feelings of frustration? It is possible that your frustrations do not originate from what happens to you but from your reactions. *If you change your reactions, you can change the way you feel.*

As an illustration, there is the true story of two sisters, one an alcoholic and the other who never drank. Their father was an alcoholic and both were asked the same question: "Why have you become the way you are?" Each gave the same explanation: "What can you expect when your father is an alcoholic?" Thus we are reminded that we are not a product of our environment, as important as the environment might be, but a product of our reactions to our environment. If you change your reactions, you can change the way you feel.

However, if you are unable to change your reactions, then reevaluate your perceptions. If you believe you have problems and feel frustrated, then one way of changing your perceptions would be to read your daily newspaper. Most likely, by page three you will read an article about someone in so much trouble that, if you could swap places, you would gladly take your problems back. You probably have never had a bad day in your life and, if you disagree, then you may need to reevaluate your perceptions of reality, of how difficult life can be. Merely by changing your perceptions of what happened, you quickly can change your reactions and, therefore, how you feel. If you cannot change your perception of what occurred, then you have one last chance, which is to reevaluate your expectations.

Behavior and Results

The last two important words to consider are *behavior* and *results*. Your results, such as how much money you earn, are by-products of how you behave and you behave according to how you feel.

Within each of us flow two rivers of feelings or emotions. One river of emotions is labeled *enthusiasm*. You are psyched and turned on and when you are on an adrenal high, your behavior will usually be courageous and risk-oriented. The results, if you remain consistent, will probably be significant.

Yet, even among the most optimistic of us exists a river of negative feelings. We refer to these emotions as *depression, despair* or *moodiness.* When these melancholy feelings take over, our behavior usually is cautious, protective and defensive. The results, at best, are minimal. Your challenge is to control the river of your own feelings.

Place an asterisk on the word feelings to remind yourself to look forward to the next day when you are frustrated. Then change what you expected was going to occur, alter your perception of what happened, or at least your reactions, and you can reshape the entire cycle.

BENEFITS OF FAILURE

Resiliency

The first benefit of failure enables you to

> ·become tougher, stronger, more resilient;
> create scar tissue on your ego; and
> temper your soul.

Once a seven-year-old boy and his brother were burned in a fire. Afterward, they shared the same bed and within three months, his brother died. Nine months later, the skin on the boy's legs had healed enough so he could walk with crutches. The first day he dropped the crutches and collapsed in horrible pain. Yet every day he forced himself through pain until, in a crippled way, he walked again. Yet he was not satisfied, because he could not run like other children, who called him "scar legs" in school. Each day, with determination, he would hold onto his horse's tail and would be dragged through the fields until he could run again; but he could not run like his friends. In his effort to be as good as average, he ran miles each day. Many years later, on the Dartmouth University track, Glen Cunningham set the world's record for the mile. Imagine what people can accomplish when they test themselves. The problem with too many people is that they have no scar tissue on their ego. They have no idea what it is to fail or to be rejected.

Just as the heat of the furnace tempers the steel, so the intensities of life's experiences strengthen your own ego. A grain of sand inside an oyster will cut the insides of the oyster, just as failure, rejection and anxiety can tear our insides. Of course, the oyster can convert the irritant into an object of beauty. Equally, you are able to convert your greatest frustrations into your greatest resiliencies.

In the same context as Glen Cunningham, consider another man who was also seven years old when an incident occurred. He was in the backyard, alone, when he saw an owl asleep in a low hanging branch. Intrigued by the idea of having his own friend, the boy quietly moved under the branch, then jumped and caught the owl by the claws. The startled owl began tearing at his arm with its beak. In pain and fear, the boy slammed the owl to the ground and killed it. Then with tears and guilt he buried the owl, thinking to himself, What can I do to make animals come alive, rather than what I've done, and make people feel happy, rather than sad? Who spent his life making animals come alive to make people happy? This is the true story of Walt Disney.

As a last example, a boy was five years old, an angelic-looking child, who lived in England. One day his father asked him to take a note to the police station. The police officer decided to follow the instructions written on the note. He took the child through a series of corridors to an open cell, locked him in and left him there. After ten minutes or so, the officer returned and explained to him, as he let him go home, "This is what happens to naughty boys." Gradually, the boy's fears caused him to become neurotic. As time passed, he realized he was becoming psychotic. Desperately, he sought a way to keep his sanity. Who spent his life creatively relieving himself of his fears? This is the true story of Alfred Hitchcock.

The stories of Glen Cunningham, Walt Disney and Alfred Hitchcock illustrate that the past is not important, but only our ability to make decisions which establish new resiliencies to resolve old feelings of inadequacy.

When a person is divorced or their business fails, does the experience cause the person to become weaker or more resilient? The choice is always ours. Most people make such decisions subconsciously, however, and too often select a negative reaction, causing anxiety, which depresses them. The next time you are disappointed, make a decision that helps you become more resilient.

Think of what factor determines success. What key quality exists within successful people that might be missing in others? Some people believe enthusiasm is that quality. Of course, it is important to be excited. Yet how valuable is enthusiasm if a person cannot handle failure?

The more emotional you are, the more effective you can be in developing rapport. Yet being emotional and enthusiastic can also increase your vulnerability to people who might be rude or hostile.

Conversely, some salespeople are unemotional and cool and analytically just present the facts. Their emotional detachment can protect them from people who are unkind or insensitive, but their lack of excitement will often reduce their ability to establish rapport.

You therefore have three choices, of which the first two are problems and the third is the solution:

1.   Be enthusiastic, develop rapport, but be vulnerable to rejection and lose your enthusiasm when people are hostile.
2.   Be emotionally detached and less likely to be upset by rejection, though people will have difficulty "warming up" to you, which may negatively impact your sales results.
3.   Or ideally, be emotionally involved and establish rapport; and when people are negative, your attitude toward rejection will keep you enthusiastic until you succeed.

A Maturing Experience

Now for the second benefit of failure. Consider the following four choices and decide which you prefer:

• Failure enhances your maturity so you are more aware of what you need to confront to succeed.
• Adversity is a learning experience.
• Rejection is the negative feedback that you need to make changes in your course of direction.
• Failure is an arena for creativity which affords you the opportunity to try new ideas.

The experience would not have been so upsetting if you had known how easily the problem could occur. You are now more familiar with how difficult this world can be.

Possibly, the only reason an experience might upset you is that it was less than what you expected. It is as though the experience now takes on a life of its own and explains, "...and you thought, just by being charming, you were going to succeed. While you are very charming, it appears you aren't quite as mature as you thought you were, since this challenge may require a little more pain and suffering than you were planning on. Don't start taking it personally and become disappointed, depressed, and defensive and want to drop out. You deserve the success. It just may require a little more frustration and anxiety before you bridge the gap."

When do you ever have a chance to try new ideas, except when you are failing? For example, imagine you are at lunch with a prospective client when you sense there are no more objections. You also realize that you have established significant rapport with this person. Are you about to try a new aggressive closing technique with someone you feel is ready to buy from you? This is probably not the time to experiment with new aggressive techniques.

So, the only chance you ever have to try new ideas is when you are failing. If you do not want any further conflict, however, you may find yourself becoming defensive. Consider these two types of people:

Those who, when they are failing, think to themselves,
O Lord, how much more must I suffer?
and those who, when failing, think to themselves,
The only opportunity I ever have to try new ideas is when I'm wiping out.

For example, a life insurance agent has just been given an aggressive closing technique. On his next appointment, he closes five times and five times the prospect is negative. He has no other techniques left to use except the new technique. So he decides to experiment. He gives the prospect a letter to sign which is made out to the agent. The prospect reads the letter: "Dear Art, I've listened to you close five times and I have firmly decided that I shall never buy any additional life insurance." "Well," the prospect says, "I'll sign it, but who would you ever show a letter like this to?" The salesman says, "I'm going to show it to your wife, after you die." This is probably an inappropriate technique to use, though the only way to decide if an approach is good or bad is to try it.

From this day on, if ever again you are disappointed by defeat, ask yourself, 'What have I learned that can make me more effective?' Too often people ask themselves, 'Why did I fail?' Yet each one of us may harbor certain doubts about ourselves, at least subconsciously. Then when we fail and think, 'Why did I do so badly?', we might begin to confirm our doubts, forget our strengths and lose our enthusiasm.

For example, Johnny comes home with a bad report card. He shows it to his mother and she says, "I'm not signing it. Give it to your father." He goes into his father's room, thinking to himself, 'Why have I done so badly? Possibly I have poor study habits. I don't care that much about school. I am lazy and maybe I'm just not that smart.' So he says, "Dad, here's my report card." His father looks at the report card and says, "Obviously, young man, you haven't been cheating!"

Yet, the longer his father looks at the card, the more hostile he becomes, until finally he says, "You have rotten study habits, you don't care about school, you're lazy and you're stupid!" When Johnny leaves the room, he no longer has any doubts. Now he believes he cannot succeed. From then on, whenever Johnny tries and fails, he will say to himself, 'I guess I'm lazy and stupid.' Whenever Johnny succeeds, he will think to himself, 'It must have been luck or an accident.'

Johnny's dad should not have negatively reinforced his son's doubts. At times, however, we are as a child, taking on a new challenge, such as starting out in selling or trying downhill skiing. On a given day, if we do badly and ask ourselves, "Why did I just mess up?", we might begin to confirm our doubts and not want to try again.

Consider Thomas Edison, who invented the light bulb but could not find a filament that would last long enough to be marketable. He tried and failed thousands of times. One day he was asked, "Mr. Edison, you have tried and failed so many times; are you discouraged?" He said, "No, I am not discouraged, because I have not failed thousands of times. I have just found thousands of different ways which do not work." Because of Edison's attitude toward failure, we have the light bulb today.

Edison failed 10,000 times before discovering a filament that would last long enough to be marketable. Yet, he always asked himself, "What did I do right, that the filament lasted as long as it did? Why did this filament last two minutes? Why did this one last five minutes? Next time, how might I make seven?"

What is your attitude toward failure? In other words, what do you think about when an experience is less than what you expected it to be? When you have not reached a desired objective within the anticipated time, what thoughts are in your mind? Your attitude toward failure determines how you feel, which influences your behavior and therefore determines your results in life.

In reality, there are only two ways to fail. One is by not trying and the other is by quitting. Otherwise you cannot fail. The experience might have been less than what you expected. However, within most experiences, which were not what you hoped they would be, there usually is some degree of success. Think of your strengths and renew your enthusiasm by asking yourself, "What did I do right that I lasted as long as I did?"

Remember the reasons why your company hired you. Recall what you did to gain your most recent account. Consider your strengths and how they have developed. Once you remember your qualities and renew your adventuresome spirit, then you are ready to try again.

Before you try, however, pause for a moment and ask another question: "Next time, what will I do to last even longer?" Succeeding on your next effort is not crucial. What is important is that you are becoming more resilient, sharpening your skills and eventually bridging the gap.

As a last life insurance example:

"This is Art Mortell with Equitable Life. Do you want to buy life insurance?" "I'm sorry Mr. Mortell, I have all I need." What did I do right to last three seconds? I found someone in, so I try again.

"This is Art Mortell with Mutual of New York. Do you want to buy life insurance?" "I'm sorry Mr. Mortell, I have all I need." "How much do you have?" "I have ten thousand dollars' worth." "Well thank you very much." What did I do right to last nine seconds? I tried a second time by asking a question. Just one new idea has multiplied my success, which encourages me to try again.

"This is Art Mortell with Prudential Insurance. Do you want to buy life insurance?" "I'm sorry Mr. Mortell, I have all I need." "How much do you have?" "I have ten thousand dollars' worth." "Then I guess you don't plan on being dead very long."

Perhaps this is an inappropriate technique. Yet the only way to decide if a technique is effective or not is to try it, and the time to try new ideas is when you are failing and you have nothing else to lose.

Motivators and Demotivators

Each of us is motivated because of our basic needs. We all want to be financially successful, achieve something of value, gain recognition, develop a positive self-image and be proud of ourselves.

Yet for every need which motivates us to set and achieve our goals is an antineed which can demotivate us to avoid our goals. These needs and antineeds can create conflict and anxiety. The more we are motivated to extend ourselves, the more our demotivators may cause us to become defensive, which is why some people may be excited to take chances, but never get started. You can probably remember when you were looking forward to achieving a particular objective and yet avoiding it at the same time.

The more precious a person, an object or an activity becomes to you, the more fearful you might become of losing it. For example, if you want to start your own business to become financially independent, you may also worry about going bankrupt and becoming financially insecure. If you want to achieve an objective, such as winning a game of tennis, you may not try for fear of losing. If you fall in love with someone, you may avoid meeting the person for fear of being rejected. If you want to discover how important you are, to develop a good self-image, you may also fear discovering that you are not as important as you think you are. If you need to gain self-esteem, you may become protective for fear that you may lose pride in yourself.

Consider the following five conflicts:

- Seeking financial self-sufficiency or avoiding financial insecurity;
- Trying to achieve an objective or avoiding failure;
- Becoming emotionally involved to gain acceptance or avoiding rejection;
- Developing your potential to gain a positive sense of identity or protecting your self-image; and

- Gaining self esteem or avoiding those challenges which might cause you to lose self-respect.

Yet, if we change our attitude toward failure, we can disengage our demotivators, resolve the inherent conflicts between our needs and antineeds and remain motivated to achieve our objectives.

As an illustration of the conflict between our desire to excel and our fear of failure, consider downhill skiing. This physical activity is quite similar to selling, for it is a cold world out there. You may also experience the humiliation of having people watch you fail in spectacular ways. If you have never tried downhill skiing, then consider the similarity of beginning in selling.

First, you are taught how to snowplow, which requires getting into a contorted position in which your knees and feet are turned inwardly. This technique keeps you in control, so you move slowly and feel secure. Next, you learn how to move sideways up a slope and then snowplow back down.

Soon you are ready for your first lift ride. The instructor shows you how to sit properly and correctly hold onto your poles and the lift. You will probably feel exhilarated as the lift carries you upward through snow-covered pine trees and granite walls. Then comes the moment to get off the lift.

You ask the person alongside you, "When do they stop this thing?", and when you are told that they do not, you feel a sense of panic, thinking to yourself, 'How will I get off this continuously moving object?'

Afterward, the lift is stopped so other skiers can drag you out of the way. These people then find your gloves, poles and hat and help you put on your skis. Next you shuffle over to the beginning of the "bunny slope," where a few minutes earlier you had exclaimed, "This looks rather flat." Now, as you stand at the top, you feel as though you are at the edge of a cliff.

You move into the snowplow position and carefully begin skiing downhill, until you take your first fall. As you lie in the cold, wet snow, watching one of your skis sliding into the wilderness while little six-year-old children who are not using poles whiz past you, you may develop a great desire to be in the bathroom. Lying in cold, wet snow may cause you to feel that way.

Reaching the bathroom in time, however, may cause only more frustration, for your hands are so cold they cannot function. This can be one of life's most humiliating moments, as you stand in the bathroom asking for help. Very embarrassing. If you think of why you are doing badly, you may only convince yourself to spend the remainder of your ski trip in the Jacuzzi.

Instead, think the same way as Thomas Edison did. Ask yourself, "What am I doing right that I am at least partially successful?" Think of how much you have learned in just three hours, as well as your courage to take on new challenges. Once you realize why you have done so well, then ask yourself, "What will I ask my instructor, on the bottom of this hill, that will reduce my falls from twelve this time to only seven next time?"

You cannot fail. Maybe the experience was not all you hoped it would be, but first ask yourself, "What did I do right that I got as far as I did?" Once you have answered that question, then ask yourself, "Next time, what will I do to do even better?"

Stepping-stones

Before discussing the third benefit of failure, think of those factors which exist in successful people that might be missing in most others. Some people claim the key factor for success is knowledge. You have probably heard the statement, "Knowledge is power," which is true to a significant extent. You will have difficulty being excited about making a presentation if you do not know what to say or feel comfortable dealing with confrontation if you have no idea what techniques to use. The more knowledgeable you are, the more confident you will feel in challenging situations. Yet consider an unusual statement: The more knowledgeable some people become, the closer they are to quitting until, as they become competent, they too often become indecisive or actually stop trying.

If this last thought sounds unusual, then think of people beginning in business. Enthusiasm is their initial quality. They are excited to begin. The one quality they are lacking is knowledge, for they are unfamiliar with the complexities of their business. Six months to a year later, they may have a reasonable degree of knowledge, but all too often they may have lost their enthusiasm, for knowledge is not power. *Only applied knowledge is power.*

Ask yourself why some people apply knowledge, but too many people, as they become more knowledgeable, actually become indecisive. Then, at the moment the person appears to be competent, he or she too often quits or becomes defensive. The problem is that these people lack one primary quality: *the ability to fail.*

Most people do not have the ability to fail. In fact, most people are so afraid of failure that they devote their entire lives to seeking comfortable situations where no risk exists. Your ability to fail and to continue trying determines your success in business or in any part of your life. Knowledge is of little value if you are unable to deal with failure.

The third benefit of failure allows you to realize that if the more you fail, the more you succeed, then what you are experiencing is not failure but only what you must go through to discover how good you are:

- Difficult times are only stepping-stones to success.
- Defeat is part of the law of averages.
- Losing is only a game you are playing that can be scored numerically.
- Adversity is a statistical, not a personal, experience.

Consider three words. The first two words are *expectations* and *reality.* The greater the gap between your expectations and reality, of where you want to be and where you are, the greater the third word: *frustration.* If ever again you are frustrated, ask yourself two questions:

- "What is reality?"
- "What are my expectations?"

Frustration usually occurs when a gap develops between where you want to be and where you are. The greater the gap, the greater the frustration.

Consistent success and positive feedback will create a positive self-image. Yet too often a person's positive self-image is based on the illusion that success is based on succeeding most of the time. Imagine if reality were to change and success were based on failing most of the time, and most people were insensitive to you. What would such experiences do to your good self-image? They might tarnish, damage or cut away at your image.

Your self-image needs to be based not on winning or losing, not on failure or success, not on love or rejection, but on your own personal sense of value. Then your self-image cannot be damaged by defeat or negative feedback. Otherwise, if you need constant success and approval of others to accept yourself, you may experience depression whenever you fail or are rejected. If your image of yourself is based on your own personaɪ sense of value, then you will be stimulated by rejection and become more resilient. Regardless of adversity, you will continue to evolve.

Think of Babe Ruth who swung a bat in a way that has not been duplicated for decades, except for Reggie Jackson. He swung so hard that when he missed, he would often fall down. In your mind's eye, you can see him, having just fallen down, covered with dirt and, on occasion, as he went back to the dugout, being booed by thousands. At that moment, he would tip his cap to the fans; and when he hit a home run, he would tip his cap to the fans. What does a man think of when being booed by thousands that he can still tip his cap to the fans? He has come to understand, "I must fail a great deal to succeed." How often must you fail before you achieve your objectives? How many times must you strike out in order to hit a home run?

Babe Ruth was famous for hitting a total of 714 home runs. Few people know that he also had 1,330 strikeouts. The reason people remember his 714 home runs but so few remember the number of strikeouts is that *people are remembered in life, not for how few times they fail, but for how often they succeed.*

Maybe there is someone you know who works very hard to make sure they don't fail. Of course, they hardly ever do fail, but then they rarely succeed. Instead, they seek comfortable situations in which there is no chance or risk of failing.

Most people have heard of Ty Cobb, a great baseball player. One of his many abilities was base stealing. In his single best year, he stole 96 bases in 134 tries. Correspondingly, few people remember Max Carey of the Pittsburgh Pirates who, in 1922, stole 51 bases in 53 tries. Why is it true that most everyone has heard of Ty Cobb and so few know of Max Carey? Again, people are remembered, not for how few times they fail, but for how often they succeed.

Many years ago, in New York, I met Lou Brock, who at that time held the record for stolen bases. He had set the record when he was about 35. I asked him, "Young players are fast with quick reflexes. How do you explain setting such a record past your prime at 35?" He said, "Art, you have to understand, when you start out in baseball, you're young and you have the speed and reflexes. When you try to steal second base and you get thrown out, it's a long walk back to the dugout, with 40,000 people watching you. However, when you reach my age, you come to understand that records are not set by being the quickest, but by the willingness to look bad in the eyes of others." Equally, you may have difficulty making presentations or using humor when speaking to a group for fear of embarrassing yourself. Yet successful people maintain a different attitude toward the challenges that most people avoid.

As a salesperson, you probably do not invest in your company. Unless you are an entrepreneur, you do not pay for the telephone, the advertising or the secretary. Yet you make the most difficult investment: You invest your ego in the business.

For example, if you are a residential real estate agent and you make 100 calls, set up three appointments, gain two listings and sell one house for $400,000, your commission (assuming that another realtor sold your listing) would be $6,000. Yet with this guaranteed formula for success, the salesperson may do this only a couple times, enjoy some success and never prospect again. The problem is that the financial success does not compensate for the emotional exhaustion caused by the 99 rejections encountered en route to the $6,000.

Therefore, your success in selling is not based on the sale but rather on your ability to persevere through the failure and rejection experienced en route to the sale. Determine the value of each adversity you must encounter to succeed by dividing the number of rejections you confront each week into your average weekly income. You will then discover how much you are paid whenever someone says no to you. With this real estate illustration, you are being paid $60 for each rejection.

In the future, whenever a prospect is hostile to you, finish the conversation by saying, "Thank you for the $60." Often the prospect will ask, "What do you mean by the $60?" This gives you the opportunity to say, "People are often rude to me, as you have been, but their rejection speeds me on to someone who needs me, and the commission I make with them I attribute to people like you, which averages about $60 every time someone says no to me."

Several benefits can be gained by using this technique:

- Aggressive people who often become irritable will usually respect people who can react to their hostility.
- Friendly people frequently become rude with people they do not know, such as a salesperson on the telephone, and when

you react with this unique blend of humor and maturity, they may become embarrassed and responsive to you.

• Most importantly, regardless of their response, this technique reinforces the basic truth that failure is only an opportunity for making money and that you are paid whenever someone rejects you.

One person's failure can be someone else's success.

Life is basically a two-step process. The first is being enthusiastic, turned on and excited. The second part of life, however, is far more crucial and that is *our ability to react under pressure.* Many people can become psyched and enthusiastic to take on a new challenge and be adventurous. But enthusiasm can be dangerous if it emotionally motivates you into a situation that you cannot deal with psychologically. You may become quickly disheartened by the adversity and emotional pressure.

You need to be enthusiastic and excited, but even more so, under pressure, you need the ability to react and persevere. Regardless of how psyched you may be, your enthusiasm is of little value if you cannot deal with failure and the stress it creates. The ability to react under pressure and continue trying become the primary factors for success.

Being excited can help you to begin. Your ability to react under pressure is even more important in ensuring your eventual success. For example, a scientist lectures in a different city each day to sophisticated people specializing in complex technology. His chauffeur travels with him and sits in the last row.

At the conclusion of one presentation, the chauffeur commented as they drove away, "Sir, I believe I have memorized your lecture so that if ever you do not feel well, I think I can give the presentation for you."

For some reason, the scientist reacted negatively to the suggestion and an argument ensued. Finally, in frustration, the scientist said, "If you think you are so capable, then you are on tomorrow morning." The chauffeur immediately agreed.

The next day, the chauffeur began the lecture, dressed in the scientist's formal tuxedo-type suit, while the scientist sat in the last row wearing the chauffeur's uniform. In fact, the chauffeur, more than having successfully memorized the presentation, was even more enthusiastic and charming.

As the applause subsided, the master of ceremonies asked the audience, "Are there any questions?" The first question was complex and profound. The chauffeur reacted immediately, as he said, "I cannot believe in an audience of this sophistication that a question so simple could be asked. In fact, to prove how simple this question is, I will have my chauffeur in the last row answer it."

He was enthusiastic to take on a new challenge, but more importantly, under pressure he was able to react.

Renews Your Humility

Now, for the fourth and last primary benefit of failure. Decide which words you prefer, for they are all the same thought:

- Failure renews your humility.
- Life is an adventure to be approached with a sense of humor.
- Adversity sharpens your objectivity.

If ever again you have a discouraging day, then remember John Glenn, presently a senator from the state of Ohio. Think back to February 20, 1962, when he was an astronaut. He was suited up and walking to the rocket ship, when a reporter asked him, "John, when you get into orbit, what's going to happen if your rockets don't fire and you can't get back down?", and he said, "It's going to spoil my day."

After John landed, the Senate held a hearing about his flight and one senator asked him, "John, what were you thinking about as you were coming back through reentry?" Glenn said, "What I was thinking about, as I was coming back through reentry, was that this capsule I was in was manufactured by the lowest bidder!" Now that could be a rather disturbing thought. Yet successful people have different attitudes toward the risk situations that most people avoid.

How objective are you for the benefit of others? You are aware of their problems and you have great solutions, whether or not you outwardly express your objectivity. Yet you might lose your objectivity for your own benefit. The problem is that you might take yourself too seriously. Therefore, if you ever start taking yourself too seriously, consider an equally unfortunate story, which might change your thinking. When you are in trouble, 80 percent of people don't even care and 20 percent are glad! While this is not a pleasant story, it is equally unpleasant if you take yourself so seriously that you lose your objectivity.

Humor is the distortion of reality.

Think of that part of reality which you feel in the morning in your lower back muscles, which by early afternoon has reached your shoulders and by late in the day may cause severe headaches. This is referred to as *anxiety, tension* and *stress.* When these toxic forms of energy graduate beyond a certain level, you may find yourself losing objectivity and becoming either depressed or irritable.

From this day on, before you allow anxiety to graduate beyond this level, stop what you are doing, step outside yourself, look back at what occurred and change your perception of what happened. When you change your perception of reality, you are forcing reality to separate, until it splits open and the tension spills out. Thus, humor is the releasing of tension.

If you distort reality too much, people might say, "That wasn't funny, that was ridiculous!" and if you do not distort reality enough people might say, "That wasn't funny, that was too serious." Your responsibility, therefore, is to catch yourself before the anxiety graduates beyond the level at which you lose objectivity. Then stop what you are doing, look back at what occurred and be amused with your own frailties. In other words, find the humor in your own frustration.

Think back to an experience that happened many years ago which was so embarrassing that you did not want anyone to know about it. As the years passed, however, it became one of your favorite stories, to be told to friends at social gatherings and to strangers in a coffee shop. What happened to change the episode from being one of the most humiliating to one of the funniest experiences of your life? What caused the transition was the element of *time.* With the passage of time, the experience began to appear as though it had happened to someone else. Therefore, speed up time!

Time travels at different speeds. When you feel depressed, time can painfully take forever. When you are enjoying yourself, time can flash on by too quickly. You can change the speed that time travels at. For example, imagine you are enjoying yourself with someone and time is moving too quickly. You want to slow down time. Just stop talking. Let the other person do all the speaking. Light the fireplace and turn on some background music. If you are alone, light a candle and stare only at it. When you physically stop moving, time will slow down. If time is moving too slowly, you may become bored and restless, so become physically active and speed up time again.

Correspondingly, you can increase the speed of time. If ever again you are depressed and time is painfully taking forever, then tell someone what occurred. When you create a war story out of a difficult experience, get the frustration off your chest or listen to a tape cassette of a comedian you enjoy, you may change your perception of what happened. In other words, find the humor in your own frailties and the amusement in your own frustrations. In these ways, you can more quickly pull yourself out of a down cycle and get back on schedule.

If you are to succeed in life, you must extend yourself and take chances. When you confront defeat, you might become disappointed. When your world is not what you hoped it would be, then the failure and rejection may cause anxiety. If you keep the anxiety inside yourself, it may weigh you down and depress you. This is a negative cycle. Rather than allow the depression to deepen, you need to speed up time by becoming amused with the person who had the bad experience, as though that person were someone else.

Comedians, to be successful, must find the amusement in their own frailties. Consider the humor of Rodney Dangerfield:

> "I didn't feel good! I went to the doctor and he said I had a virus. I said, 'I want a second opinion.' So he said, 'You're ugly, too!'

> "And last month, we had a fire in the house. My kids were yelling, 'Fire, fire,' and my wife was telling them, 'Shut up! Dad's sleeping!' I'll tell ya. No respect! I sent my picture to a lonely hearts club. They mailed it back. They said, 'We're not that lonely!'

> "I said to my psychiatrist, 'I got suicidal tendencies.' Now he's billing me in advance!"

What Rodney Dangerfield does for us, we need to do for ourselves each day. We need to find the humor in our own frailties and the amusement in our frustrations.

Think of how failure helps you to develop your potential. In other words, how does failure enhance your self-image? Consider the positive relationship between failure and self-esteem. For most of us, a day will come that is not all we hoped it would be. On that day, remember why *you need failure in your life to develop your potential, enhance your self-image and gain self-esteem.*

We live in a society that believes that winning is not the most important thing, that winning is the only thing. Of course, winning is the best experience of all. Success is exciting and satisfying. Yet it is possible that success might be dangerous and failure is always positive. Think of how success can lead to boredom, apathy and letdowns.

For example, George Sanders was a British actor. He enjoyed wealth, fame, recognition and financial independence. He also married beautiful women, such as Zsa Zsa Gabor. When George achieved all his goals in life, he gave himself a promised gift—retirement to his lovely villa in Spain. Then he shot himself in the head. His brief suicide note revealed that he had decided to leave because he had become so bored. It is unfortunate that a person should ever become so successful and so satisfied to become so bored and depressed.

Be careful of success, for that which is the best experience in life can often be the most dangerous. Once again, success can lead to boredom, lethargy, loss of objectivity, lack of humility and egotism. You can depend on failure, however, for whenever you try to succeed, failure will be waiting for you. Therefore, make failure a good friend. Find time each day to ask failure how it has helped you become more resilient. Allow adversity to renew your humility and sharpen your objectivity. Just one thought can change your attitude toward failure, your perception of reality, your expectations of yourself and, therefore, your results.

2

Being Amused by Rejection

"Have the ability to be, not the person you are, but the person you need to be."

Before discussing the solution to rejection, consider a transitional question: Is it possible that rejection might be a more negative experience than failure? For many people, failure would not be so upsetting if no one knew about it. Usually, the problem is not in adversity, but in the humiliation. For example, you send out 100 pieces of direct mail, but you do not get a response. Does that upset you? Probably not.

Then you call on your best prospect. You feel a significant rapport with this person. You ask him for his decision and he says, "I'm sorry. I am buying from someone else, but I want you to know that I think you are a nice person. However, I decided to buy from someone else because I question your competence and knowledge. In fact, I think you're somewhat stupid." Now that probably would bother you for a few hours or maybe even a couple days.

A lack of response from direct mail might not upset you because there is no emotional involvement to cause you to feel personally rejected. Then why would the last situation frustrate you? The reason: The more emotionally involved you become with someone, the more you begin to subconsciously assume that the other person knows you better than you know yourself, for they can see you more easily than you can see yourself. Therefore, they can more objectively compare you to others, causing you to feel vulnerable to any potential rejection and invariably defensive.

As an illustration of this last thought, imagine meeting someone in your personal life. The person says, "I love you. I want to spend the rest of my life with you." This tends to enhance your self-image. You become involved with the person, experiencing love, intimacy and marriage; and the years pass. Then you wake up one morning and your spouse says, "I now feel that I know you very well and I don't love you anymore." This is referred to as *rejection*.

What period of time is required for the ego to heal from the trauma of this experience? At least six months, if not a few years. The desire to be involved again usually motivates the person into entering another relationship. Then, within their subconscious mind, a voice says, "Watch out, you might get hurt again."

At that moment, you may begin to self-destruct the relationship. If the relationship is not meaningful, it might last forever. Yet the more important the other person becomes, the more vulnerable you are to rejection. For many people, the solution is to end the relationship. The result is that you destroy what you might need most of all. This problem can also occur each day in business, for the more involved you become with someone, the more concerned you are of how the person feels about you and the more cautious you may become in your behavior.

TAKING REJECTION PERSONALLY

There are two kinds of rejection. One type of rejection happens to be an amusing experience. You can tell your friends what occurred. The incident might even seem funny to you. The second kind of rejection can cause a person who has failed, in a job or marriage, to never try the same challenge again. Obviously, the second kind of rejection is quite dangerous.

Only one word determines the difference between rejection which is amusing and rejection which is dangerous to your ego and that single word is *personal*. If you do not take the rejection personally, then you are not upset. You might even laugh about it. Taking rejection personally, however, may damage your ego. More specifically, it can damage your self-image.

For example, you stop for a red light and notice in the car alongside you that the person is sticking their tongue out at you. Does that upset you? Of course not. You think to yourself, 'This person must have some type of problem.' Yet under what circumstances might such an experience upset you? What if you knew the person? What if it was your spouse or your manager? What if it was your spouse and manager together? What if other people had reacted negatively toward you earlier in the day? You might start wondering, What's wrong with me?, which is a dangerous question to ask yourself.

How Emotionally Involved?

Rejection is taken personally for three reasons. The first reason is *emotional involvement*. The question, again, is *how emotionally involved can I become with someone before I assume that the person knows me so well that whatever he or she says might be true, causing me to feel vulnerable to rejection and, therefore, to be defensive?*

Imagine becoming involved with someone who reacts negatively to you. This might not upset you, because you think to yourself, This person cannot reject me if he doesn't know me. As an illustration, if you make prospecting calls on the telephone and a person is rude, that might not frustrate you, for you can think to yourself, If this person had seen my face, he or she would have accepted me, so I don't feel rejected.

Yet if you were halfway into a one-hour face-to-face appointment and the prospect were to say, "The more I get to know you, the more I dislike you. I want you to leave," this probably would upset you.

Each one of us needs to progress through varying levels of responsibilities where at each level, we may confront a greater intensity of rejection that often creates our own limitations. Evaluate your ability to progress through each of these challenges:

- You can send out direct mail but feel uncomfortable prospecting;
- You can make prospecting calls but feel inhibited during appointments and therefore avoid face-to-face conversation;
- You can meet people but are reluctant to ask for the order; or
- You can ask for the order and persevere until you gain the sale but not call afterward for fear the client may have developed negative feelings.

You need to develop an effective relationship with the prospect if you are to achieve the desired results. The more you become involved with people so they will trust you, however, the more concerned you might become that they will reject you.

Think of how well you know yourself. Assume that at this time your self-image is relatively high and you are feeling good about yourself. Then the subject of emotional involvement appears. As long as your self-image is greater than your emotional involvement, you will not take the rejection personally. Rather, you will think to yourself, How can this person reject me, when they don't even know me? or If this person knew me, they would like me.

Yet, at the point when your emotional involvement begins to exceed your self-image, all the assumptions in your subconscious mind may begin to change: 'I think this person knows me very well. They can see me more easily than I can see myself and compare me to others more objectively. If this person were to reject me, I might take it personally. Therefore, I will do nothing to antagonize this person.' At that point, you may become cautious in your behavior.

Almost every one of us is vulnerable to reaching a level of involvement in which we might start taking rejection personally, allowing our self-image to be damaged and our feelings to be hurt.

Each of us has a self-image. On those days when we are feeling good about ourselves and our self-image is very strong, we will feel comfortable taking chances. However, if we take failure or rejection personally, our self-image may weaken and we might become cautious. Our involvement with people may become minimal, causing us to "chill out."

Do you know anyone who is gregarious and charming with people who are only friends or acquaintances but in their most important relationships often becomes protective or even begins to self-destruct the relationship? When we begin to depend on the other person to feel good about ourselves then, to avoid such dependency and the danger of being hurt, we become defensive.

How emotionally involved can you become with someone before you take their negative feedback personally (see Figure 2.1)? How might that affect your relationships, not just in business but in your personal life? You need to be aware of that moment in a relationship when you become too concerned with the reactions of the other person. Then you need to decide what you will do to pursue your objective, such as asking for the order, even though you feel vulnerable to any possible rejection.

Figure 2.1   Measuring Rejection

Relationship Between Emotional Involvement and Self-Image

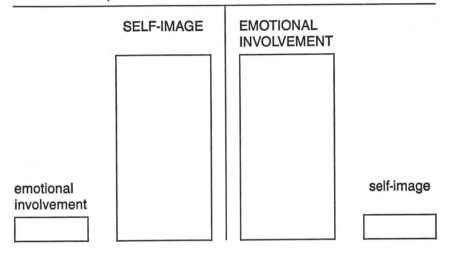

How Much Rejection?

The second reason rejection is taken personally is the quantitative or numerical factor. In other words, *how much failure and rejection can you experience before you start taking it personally?* Of course, you can handle rejection. One of the reasons why you are as successful as you are is that you can deal with rejection. The question is, how much rejection can you experience before even you begin taking it personally?

More specifically:

- How many prospecting calls can you make before the negative reactions upset you?
- How many times will you follow up on a qualified prospect before you decide the possible results do not justify the constant negative feedback?
- How many times will you close before you do not want to confront any further resistance?

While the life insurance agent may confront rejection when prospecting and the computer sales representative may be discouraged when losing a large order, the stockbroker may experience the greatest rejection. When the price of the stock declines, then clients may call the broker and ask, "What have I ever done to you that you would want to do this to me?" Brokers usually will feel especially rejected when they have to call their mother and say, "Mom, this a margin call. You're short." And she says, "What is a margin call?" "Mom, you owe more money. The firm can't carry you." Then she says, "I carried you for nine months; can't you carry me for one more week?"

Yet being a financial consultant can create the opportunity for great financial success. Many stockbrokers earn more than $250,000 a year in net income, often on a relaxed schedule. Their administrative assistant or secretary does most of their work, such as calming an angry client, coordinating research and preparing paperwork, while the broker devotes a major part of the day to having breakfast and lunch with their favorite clients to gain referrals and repeat business and to sell diversified products.

For the broker to do well financially, with minimal failure, rejection and anxiety, however, requires developing a significant number of clients. If the broker calls on quality people, then approximately 500 clients might justify the transition from cold calling to referral selling, generating repeat business and marketing diversified products.

Usually, ten cold-call conversations should net one prospect and five prospects will result in one new account. Using these mathematics, 50 cold-call conversations should net one new account and 25,000 prospecting calls should result in 500 clients and a significant income without significant stress. Yet of these 25,000 conversations, 24,500 will be hostile, negative and resistant.

Therefore, the primary factor for success in selling is being stimulated by the rejection which most people avoid.

You need to remind yourself that failure and rejection do not exist. Rather, you are playing a game of percentages. Disengage that part of your personality that is oversensitive and merely keep score of how many people will say no before someone buys from you.

In 1982, Ricky Henderson set the single-season stolen-base record of 130. Few people know that he also set the record for being caught 42 times. How many times must you "wipe out," and often feel embarassed, to succeed?

In the same year, Pete Rose set the record for most hits in a career. Few people know that he also set the record for most times out in a career. Remember that you are playing a statistical game in which you keep score of those factors which determine your success.

Realize that you have a "guaranteed formula for success." Whenever I need to book a lecture, I know that if I call a certain number of prospects, I will gain interest among a given percentage which will net one confirmed speech. If you have yet to determine the numbers within your formula for success, then begin playing the game. There is no rejection when every effort is only a statistical experience.

There is, however, a difference between failing and being wrong. When Pete Rose made outs, he did not fail since the experience was only part of the process of succeeding. As mentioned previously, if the more you fail, the more you succeed, then you cannot refer to the experience as failure but only what you must go through to maximize your own performance.

Pete Rose went to jail, nevertheless, not because he failed, but because he was wrong. You must separate failing from being wrong. Failure is a positive experience for it stimulates your adventuresome spirit to rise to the challenge. Being wrong challenges you to make corrections within the values of your character. Otherwise, what you plant grows only weeds.

Rejection from Whom?

The third and last reason why you take rejection personally is based on the person who is rejecting you. Are there people in your life who make you feel inadequate? Possibly, their age, position or title causes you to believe that whatever they say might be true, including their opinion of you.

More specifically, most of us are charismatic with people who cause us to feel comfortable. With such people we are both aggressive and friendly. Why, then, could we lose the charismatic balance in which we continue to be warm and friendly but are not aggressive nor confident? Somehow we have decided that these people are superior to us so that whatever they say must be true, which causes us to be vulnerable to any potential rejection.

In another perspective, you have three personalities. Your first personality is the way you are with people who you feel are beneath you. You might not want to admit to such social snobbery. If you are invited to a party, however, you might find an excuse not to go, claiming, "They're not my kind of people. I might get bored."

As another example, if you are walking along the street and you disregard someone who asks you for a quarter and he curses you as you walk away, does that bother you? Probably not, because in your mind this person is not a judge of what you are worth. Your first personality, therefore, is the way you are with people you feel are beneath you.

Your second personality is the way you are with people who you feel are your equal. With these people you are both aggressive and friendly. You are in charismatic balance. These people, if they were critical of you, would cause you to think to yourself, 'Maybe I am not as important as I want to think I am. Yet, since I am as good as this person, I should realize that their criticism is feedback that can help me make changes in the direction of my course. This is an opportunity to improve myself!' Thus, negative feedback from these people may cause you to introspect, to determine where you need to change to deal more effectively with similar situations in the future.

The third part of your personality is the way you react to people who make you feel uncomfortable. With such people you may become cautious and defensive.

As an illustration of our three personalities, think of the old television program, "The Honeymooners," with Jackie Gleason. Ralph had three personalities. With his wife Alice and his friend Ed Norton, he could be insensitive and abusive. With his friends at work he was gregarious, charming and charismatic. With his boss he was shy and apprehensive. Can you see yourself in these same patterns?

If you understand the relationship between your self-image and your opinions of others, you may recognize why you are comfortable with some people and uncomfortable with others. Your challenge is to disengage from your unconscious reaction, which may be self-defeating, and develop patterns which improve your effectiveness and therefore your self-image.

Think of your reactions to rejection which are preventing you from achieving your objectives. Consider those people who cause you to feel inadequate and apprehensive. Take control of the process by recognizing the choices of behavior which are available to you and making the correct decision.

For example, in a seminar I was conducting, a life insurance agent admitted that he had a poor self-image and that his success in life had been minimal until he began selling insurance. Suddenly, he was calling on doctors, lawyers and executives and doing very well financially. He was an exception to the 62 percent of new life insurance agents who fail during their first year. He was also an exception to those agents who succeed by calling on newlyweds and if they are rejected, think to themselves, 'How can this person reject me? I'm as good as they are.' While they do succeed, their income is somewhat limited. I was interested in knowing why this agent was able to call on important people despite his poor self-image, so I asked him, "How can you feel comfortable contacting people who are so successful?" He said, "I think to myself, if I am going to be rejected all day long, let it be from someone important." Merely by changing his attitude toward failure, he had changed his entire reaction to rejection.

In review, what do you think about when you fail? When you are rejected, how do you react?

In 1972, an IBM sales representative contacted me. He had just been assigned a territory of 50 qualified prospects, with no existing customers. He felt comfortable contacting 48 of the prospects, but he did not understand why he was avoiding two prospective customers.

During the conversation, he told me that the 48 he was contacting were small companies and the decision makers were purchasing agents and accountants. The two companies he was avoiding were large and, according to the previous sales representative, the contact within both companies was the president.

I asked him how he felt when calling on purchasing agents of small companies and he said, "No problem. I feel I am as good as they are."

Then I asked him why he was avoiding these two major prospects. After a long pause, he said, "I feel that anyone who is the president of a company of that size must be a very important person and just the thought of calling on someone at that level makes me apprehensive."

Yet with that honesty he made the calls and went well over his quota.

In summary, if we fail but no one knows it, then the failure is not that serious. For many of us, *it is not the failure that upsets us, but the rejection.* In other words, the humiliation is the problem. Why do you think you may take rejection personally? Is it because you have been rejected a number of times in a row or because the person who is rejecting you is important to you? If the rejection is from someone you feel is not equal to you, it may not bother you. If you feel that the person is your equal, you may take it seriously. If you feel the person is more important than you are, then you may take their negative feedback too much to heart.

Courage

From Rollo May's book *Courage to Create* comes the idea that an acorn automatically becomes an oak tree, just as a kitten becomes a cat, but we do not become the person we were designed to be by instinct. For us, the process of developing our potential requires a different ingredient, which is *courage*. This quality has two parts. First, we need the courage to be *honest* with ourselves. It is not easy to admit our own frailties. Often it is difficult to admit the reasons why we take failure and rejection personally.

The second part is the courage *to suffer*. In other words, we need to be willing to experience failure, rejection and anxiety to bridge the gap from where we are to where we need to be. If we can capitalize on stress, we can develop our potential, enhance our self-image and increase our self-esteem.

Why Do You Take Rejection Personally?

Following are three reasons why you may take rejection personally:

Frequency

When adversity occurs more frequently than you expected, you may assume that you are the cause of your misfortune, rather than objectively realizing that the frequency of failure might be a normal occurrence.

Emotional Involvement

When you feel that someone has a greater awareness of who you are than you have of yourself, you may assume that their opinion of you is valid, causing you to feel vulnerable to any negative comments, thus creating emotional limitations in which your objective might be to protect your ego rather than extend yourself.

The Person

If you respect the other person more than yourself, then you may believe what he or she says, causing you to take personally any negative comment this person may have of you. You need to understand that your fears and vulnerabilities create your limitations. Yet if you can attack your fears, then your vulnerabilities also can stimulate you to break through your psychological barriers.

We now will convert these factors, of why we take rejection personally, into three challenges, in which we can "stretch ourselves" and become more successful.

THE THREE CHALLENGES OF SELLING

Massive Prospecting

You need to meet all potential customers, make their acquaintance and determine if and when they might need you. At the beginning of a sales career, your objective, of continuous cold calling, is crucial until you have established enough clients to justify moving on to the next stage.

Emotional Involvement

If you want your clients to be good references, give you referrals and repeat business, as well as allow you to explore additional applications for marketing diversified products, then you need to create a unique involvement that moves you beyond your competitors. If, for example, you are selling financial services, have lunch with your client and meet with their accountant.

Think of the percentage of your clients who might prefer that you call them on the weekend when they are more relaxed and the relationship becomes one of friendship rather than business. Then, more easily, you can ask questions and determine their objectives.

Upgrade Your Market

Call on people of importance. If you are marketing computer services, call on the top decision makers and focus on major projects which are most profitable. If you are a stockbroker, contact the most important people and increase your gross income per ticket.

PSYCHOLOGICAL SOLUTIONS TO REJECTION

The first solution to rejection is psychological. As an analogy, ducks and geese can avoid becoming wet in a rainstorm in the same two ways in which you can avoid becoming depressed by rejection. There is one option you do not want, however, and that is to hide or seek shelter. In other words, think of the two ways that you can continue moving in a storm, toward your target, and not become depressed by the rain. How do ducks and geese do it?

They fly above the clouds, and your solution is to raise your self-image. You need to fly above the adversity of life and the hostility of others. When you decide, I am a child of God, I am precious and of value, then the rejection, whether valid or invalid, is always for your benefit.

If the rejection is valid, you need to understand why you have caused this person's reaction. You need the negative feedback so as to make changes in the direction of your course. Then there is invalid rejection, in which the person is taking their frustrations out on you.

If ever again a person is negative toward you, ask, "Could you tell me what I said to upset you, so that I will not make the same error in the future, or are you having a bad day and just taking your frustrations out on me?" Whether the rejection is valid or invalid, you need to understand the cause of their hostility. Only then can you capitalize on these negative feelings and become more effective.

The second way to deal with rejection is "raindrops off a duck's feathers." In other words, if you cannot fly above the rejection, then "disengage your ego." The preferable solution is to *raise your self-image,* so that rejection, whether valid or invalid, is always for your benefit. In this way, you can be both emotionally and ego-involved. Understand that your self-image lives in your ego. If you begin taking rejection personally, then your self-image is in danger of becoming damaged. To protect your self-image, you need to detach your ego yet stay emotionally involved.

Can you be emotionally involved with someone while at the same time being ego-detached? Not easily, but it can be accomplished. For example, have you recently seen a movie that was both true and traumatic? Consider the three types of people who watch movies. When violence and trauma occur, the first person says, "It's only a movie! That's called special effects. That person is being paid to go through that." The second person is temporarily traumatized and permanently damaged.

Hopefully, you are the third person who becomes emotionally involved with the movie and feels what is happening, but is not touched, traumatized or overwhelmed by it. The objective is to become so fascinated with human behavior, particularly the origins of hostility, that if ever again a person is angry with you, you extend yourself just to determine why. Your curiosity causes you to become more emotionally involved, while your desire to understand their negative feeling disengages your ego, so your self-image is protected.

As another analogy, consider the wind. You cannot see the wind, nor can you touch it. Yet you can feel the wind and it has power. It can uproot trees and carry away houses and cars. You want to become the wind. You want to feel what people feel, but they cannot touch you. You want to move people, but they cannot hurt you. Understand that a primary quality in successful people that is missing in most others is the ability *to be the person you need to be, not the person you are.*

Managing Yourself

Before discussing the second major solution to rejection, which is the behavioral solution, consider the topic of managing yourself. There are three parts of our life in which we need to manage ourselves. These three involve how we *think, feel* and *behave.* First, we need to think positively if we are to be consistently confident and enthusiastic. Yet, interestingly, positive thinking frequently can be dangerous. This is because if we do not recognize the potential for defeat, then we will be unprepared for the reality we may need to confront. We need to understand how our optimism can blind us to possible repercussions.

Sometimes we might do better if we think negatively. More specifically, think of two words: procrastination and panic. Do you ever procrastinate? Think back to your college days when a term-paper assignment was due. Often students began working on it the night before. Then by sunrise, on caffeine and candy bars, they often were brilliant!

Panic breaks procrastination.

Negative thinking can be healthy if it creates a sense of urgency which forces us to become productive. Thus, positive or negative thinking is not our concern. What is important is *our ability to manage our thinking.* You need to capitalize on your thinking. Sometimes negative thinking can stimulate you into productive patterns.

Negative thinking creates anxiety, and some people *manage the anxiety* effectively. More specifically, they convert anxiety into a creative force for achievement, which keeps them in continuous motion until they succeed. By channeling the anxiety into productive activities, they become more effective. You can think negatively, therefore, and positively manage the stress.

Yet if you think and feel negatively you can still succeed. You have one last chance. If you do not effectively manage the way you think and feel, then you need to *manage the way you behave*—thus, the behavioral solution to rejection.

Two Negative Reactions

There are two negative reactions to rejection. If you understand which of these two reactions you most likely will use with people who are hostile toward you, then you may recognize the solution. The first negative reaction to rejection is the most popular, and used most frequently, which is to stop trying. With this negative reaction, you become oversensitive and cautious and retreat.

The second negative reaction to rejection that occurs less frequently but is more provocative is to counterattack and "straighten people out." Which way do you react to rejection? If you are not sure, then try the following test. Assuming that you read the "Peanuts" cartoon, which person would you prefer to be if your only choices were Charlie Brown or Lucy?

If you prefer to be Charlie, then you probably are the warm, sensitive type who easily develops rapport with people. You can tell Charlie whatever you want and he never will use it against you. However, Charlie is so afraid of rejection from the little red-haired girl, that he cannot even talk to her. Then there is Lucy, who has no problem taking the initiative. She will persevere forever, but she often is insensitive and upsets others.

Do you know anyone similar to Charlie, who is loving and kind but often is oversensitive and takes rejection too much to heart? Such people usually avoid confrontation, can be taken advantage of and become depressed when people are cruel. Then there are people such as Lucy, who, merely on the suspicion that someone may insult them, will attack first. Finally, do you know anyone who is like Snoopy—flying above the clouds, fighting the Red Baron, with no idea of what really is happening? However, they are happy people!

How do you react to rejection? Do you become oversensitive and defensive like Charlie Brown or counterattack and become hostile like Lucy? Maybe you are like Snoopy, who is oblivious to what is occurring and disregards the rejection. Now, what changes would you make in the way you deal with rejection to become more successful?

Charisma

The solution to rejection is based on one word, which is *charisma*. The definition: *Charisma is the balancing of opposite qualities into such a personality that almost anyone can identify with you.* What qualities would you need to develop to create that balance? You can create charisma for yourself if you answer two questions.

First, what do you believe is Charlie Brown's primary quality? Second, what do you feel is Lucy's primary strength? Take these two words and rephrase them, using Lucy's word first. For example, attack nicely or react pleasantly. As an exercise in developing charismatic balance, select one quality from each of the following two columns:

aggressively	friendly
confidently	sensitive
persistently	humble

tenaciously	warm
decisively	compassionate
relentlessly	pleasant
assertively	kind

For instance, be *aggressively sensitive, relentlessly compassionate* and *tenaciously warm*. What you thought were weaknesses or liabilities become strengths when balanced with capitalizing qualities.

As a personal illustration, there was a time in my life when I was insecure. I was 13, had just begun high school, was shy and defensive. I was afraid to try dancing. I could not speak in front of a class. I would not ask a girl for a date.

I began to realize that the origin of my problem was my reactions to my parents. I identified with my mother, who was sensitive and loving, as well as quiet and reserved. I could not relate to my father, however, who was aggressive and dominant. I felt he was insensitive to me. I decided I would be as my mother, for then people would feel positive toward me, as I felt toward her. I also decided not to be like my father, for I would not want people seeing me as aggressive and insensitive.

Therefore, for fear of being like my father, I avoided confrontation. I would speak only when spoken to and I became inhibited.

Then I saw the movie "To Kill a Mockingbird." In the movie, Gregory Peck is very aggressive when dealing with such challenges as racial prejudice, a rabid dog and hostile people. Yet he was aggressive in a calm and gentle way.

Suddenly I realized that sensitivity can be a liability if it is not tempered with resiliency, and aggressiveness can be disarming if it is softened by kindness and gentleness. Obviously, balance is the answer.

3

Thriving on Anxiety

Happiness is based on modifying your expectations to keep yourself in balance.

Selling can be very stressful. Yet if you allow stress to stimulate you into creating patterns of success, you may easily achieve your objectives. Recognize the direct relationship which exists between your ability to capitalize on stress and your effectiveness in a marketing responsibility.

If you react positively to stress and anxiety, your primary frustration might be boredom. The solution, then, is to take on greater challenges to increase the stress so that you feel stimulated again.

THE BENEFITS OF ANXIETY

Anxiety provides two primary benefits. Before discussing the first benefit of anxiety, think of how every part of our world works for our benefit. For example, pain has been given to us as a present. If you could not experience pain, you could be damaging yourself and never know it. So pain is good, for it tells you that you are moving in the wrong direction.

Certain children, unfortunately, are born without being able to feel pain. Someone must always be watching them, for if they were cut and bleeding or had their hands on a hot stove, they would be unaware that they were hurting themselves. Just as pain warns us that we are in danger, so emotional pain and anxiety are early warn-

41

ing signals. Pain asks us to stop what we are doing to determine what is causing it. Anxiety is our psychological pain, which asks us to stop what we are doing to determine the origins of our frustration.

Isolate Your Vulnerability

The first benefit of anxiety is that it can help you *isolate your vulnerability*. The primary reason you become upset is because of a vulnerability within you which has yet to be resolved. Think of how your frustrations are reflections of your self-image. For example, if you allow a problem which is petty to upset you, then obviously you are not thinking very much of yourself.

For example, most successful salespeople become frustrated when dealing with paperwork. They feel that filling out forms is too petty. Then there are the challenges which excite us, such as prospecting, making a presentation or closing. Yet certain responsibilities, such as dealing with an aggressive, dominant decision maker of a major account, may cause us to feel vulnerable.

We, therefore, have three situations, of which the first and last usually will frustrate us:

1. Petty situations which we feel are beneath our self-image;
2. Situations which we enjoy because they challenge and stimulate us without overwhelming us; and
3. Difficult situations which threaten our self-image.

From this day on, if you are ever again frustrated, think back to the last moment when you felt good. Then think of the moment when you became frustrated and decide what happened to upset you. Isolate the moment when the anxiety began and realize that what occurred was a catalyst which irritated an unresolved vulnerability.

Energy for Continuous Movement

The second benefit of anxiety is to understand that anxiety is energy which is toxic only if internalized. In other words, if you keep the stress within yourself, it may negatively motivate you into self-destructive behavior. You may become depressed and defensive, or hostile and abusive. When the anxiety is used instead as a force for achievement, however, it can power you through the obstacles which most people avoid. Thus, the second benefit of anxiety is *energy for continuous movement.*

As an illustration, consider the only two types of animals which exist in our world: predators and those that are preyed on. In other words, hunters and those which are hunted, and literally eaten alive. Notice that those who are hunted include big animals, such as elks, horses and cows, and tiny animals, such as mice, rabbits and squirrels.

Predatory animals are wolves, coyotes, lions, tigers and people. You may not like the idea that we are physiologically and instinctively conditioned to enjoy the hunt. You may need to accept this inherent part of your nature, however, to understand why you experience anxiety so easily. Turtles experience very little stress. Cows and sheep are relaxed animals. Yet we quickly can become irritable when we are not where we want to be.

How do you deal with stress? Too often, people keep the anxiety inside themselves, which causes depression and despair. This negatively motivates them to avoid any further challenges for fear of experiencing additional frustration. Instead we need to convert the anxiety into some form of activity which enhances our self-image. Eliminate the valleys and cause the peaks to become more frequent, so you are consistently on target. Channel anxiety into a force for achievement.

For example, an aborigine in Australia today still hunts the kangaroo as he has hunted for thousands of years. At the first color of dawn, he takes up the hunt and chases the kangaroo. He cannot catch it, but he chases it all day long. When darkness comes and he has no idea where the kangaroo has gone, he falls asleep. The kangaroo, realizing it is no longer being hunted, soon stops moving and falls asleep.

The next morning, at sunrise, the aborigine resumes the hunt. The kangaroo hears him coming and starts running again, but has difficulty moving. The kangaroo never has had to run for an entire day as it did the day before. Its ligaments, cartilage and muscles have stiffened up. It is unable to move quickly. The aborigine continues moving steadily, kills the kangaroo and carries him back.

Our instinctive nature is to be on the move continuously until we have channeled the anxiety into achieving what causes us to feel comfortable. For this reason, the next time you are in a social gathering and someone asks you what kind of work you do, be honest and tell them, "I'm a hunter and gatherer." Return to your inherent nature. You are on the move again. When you become frustrated, do not keep the stress inside of yourself and become depressed. Instead, channel the anxiety into a creative force of energy and become more productive.

Today, in our civilization, certain groups experience a high rate of suicide. One group is dentists. You think your job is difficult and frustrating? Try working in people's mouths, which are not the prettiest places to be. Dentists also want to make you feel better by doing a good job so that you will appreciate them. Yet, all they see in the eyes of their patients is the thought, 'I hate being here.' They also want to talk to you, so they ask you questions which you cannot answer.

Many people, who have not developed positive ways to react to anxiety, keep the anxiety within themselves, feel weighed down and overwhelmed by this negative pressure and are often in danger of suicide.

In review, there are two problems in life: the problem and the anxiety which the problem creates. If you can eliminate the problem before the frustration has caused anxiety, then you can protect yourself from becoming seriously depressed or hostile. If an awareness of your vulnerabilities does not solve the problem, however, then you need to understand how to channel the anxiety creatively and productively.

THE SOLUTIONS TO ANXIETY

Now for the solution regarding anxiety. First, acknowledge that you do not enjoy excessive stress. Experiencing emotional pressure is no fun. When you encounter toxic energy, you may seek devices that relieve you of the irritation. When you find a technique that effectively eliminates the tension, you may become so dependent on that anxiety-eliminating technique that you literally become addicted to it.

People self-destructively use ten negative addictions to cope with stress, which hurt their health, reduce longevity, neutralize their energy, decrease their endurance and vitality, create a negative impact on people, cut them off from reality, reduce creativity, damage their self-image and reduce self-esteem, as well as their results in life.

People also employ four positive addictions to deal with anxiety. These positive addictions do not cause you to cope with stress. The word *cope* is too ineffective. They cause you to *thrive* on stress. They give you a sense of achievement, help you confront reality and improve your impact on people. They increase energy, endurance, longevity and vitality, while improving your health. They sharpen creativity, enhance your self-image and increase self-esteem, as well as your results in life.

The Negative Addictions

The ten negative addictions are:

1. Smoking,
2. Alcohol,
3. Caffeine,
4. Food,
5. Television,
6. Oversleeping,
7. Drugs,
8. Gambling,
9. Depression or
10. Hostility.

All negatives are either uppers or downers. In other words, uppers stimulate you and keep you moving, while downers pacify you.

Also recognize that the only two causes of stress are *boredom* and *burnout*. Both are caused by *expectations*. If your expectations are too high, you are vulnerable to burnout. In other words, you are in danger of becoming overwhelmed and short-circuiting. If your expectations are too low, your vulnerability could be boredom. Therefore, *happiness is based on modifying your expectations to keep yourself in balance.*

Consider these two words. The first is *stimulated,* such as being turned on and excited. The second word is *mellow,* such as being comfortable, relaxed and content. In review, you want to raise your expectations to be stimulated. If you demand too much of yourself, however, you might find yourself in danger of burnout. Then you need to lower your expectations—take a long weekend, read a book, remain calm. Yet, if you become too relaxed, you might become bored. You need to enjoy the highs of being stimulated and the lows of being mellow, yet avoid the boredom and burnout reactions. (See Figure 3.1.)

Figure 3.1   Energy Zones

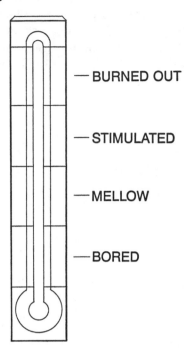

— BURNED OUT

— STIMULATED

— MELLOW

— BORED

Now merge two separate thoughts: boredom and burnout and uppers and downers. The people who hate boredom and need to be stimulated often will self-destructively depend on uppers. These people enjoy being hyper, love crises and often become irritable. Then there are people who try to tranquilize and pacify their mind, body and ego to avoid reality. These people too often will self-destructively depend on downers to escape the pressure of their own responsibilities. They tend to be oversensitive and vulnerable and want to avoid confrontation. For example, hyper-type salespeople, when frustrated, often will become irritable with a secretary, while those who are passive may go to an afternoon movie.

At this time, review the ten negative addictions and score them as uppers or downers. Also note that two are both uppers and downers. Then decide which of these negatives you most depend on.

In review, smoking is an upper. Nicotine constricts the blood vessels, which reduces the flow of oxygen to the brain. The brain, depleted of oxygen, sends a message to your adrenal glands to release adrenaline into the heart to increase the flow of blood so as to compensate for the depletion of oxygen. The heart is now beating, on average, 22 percent faster than usual. Smoking is, therefore, an upper for those who hate depression, cannot tolerate mental fatigue and find in a single cigarette the equivalent of a fast shot of adrenaline, thus a stimulant.

Alcohol is a downer. Alcohol is not a relaxant, but rather a depressant. It is for those who want to tranquilize their ego from reality. The reason some people think it is an upper is that alcohol can bring us down below our inhibitors, so that we no longer care what the reactions of others might be. We become spontaneous, such as expressing our fears and anger or telling silly stories. Again, such reactions occur only because we have become so relaxed that we do not care what others think of us.

Caffeine is an upper. People depend on coffee to get them started in the morning and keep them alert throughout the day and also at night. Yet caffeine does not give us energy. The reason why coffee stimulates us is that it is a drug in the amphetamine category. However, while quickly stimulating us, it also depletes energy, causing letdown afterwards, as well as making us hungrier, more tired and vulnerable to depression. Caffeine also causes hyper-type reactions, increases the heartbeat and disrupts the time clocks within our physiological system, such as eating and sleeping cycles. In addition, coffee causes panic attacks among 15 percent of the population, has been linked to certain forms of cancer and heart disease and creates nervousness within most everyone.

Many people who drink caffeinic beverages, but do not believe that they are addicted to caffeine, might want to experiment and avoid it for a few days. A large percentage of people will experience a variety of withdrawal reactions, such as having difficulty awakening in the morning or staying awake throughout the day, as well as having frequent headaches.

Food is both an upper and a downer. One type of an upper food is sugar which has been processed by machines, refined and is ready to be digested immediately. This requires an insulin reaction which quickly, though temporarily, gives you a fast high. Downer-type foods take hours to digest, causing you to become groggy, sleepy and sluggish. These are fat and protein, such as meat, eggs, cheese, whole milk, creams, sauces, butter and ice cream.

The ideal food is complex carbohydrates, which include three items: natural grains, vegetables and fruit. These foods have two important ingredients. One is fiber, which digests rapidly, causing your mind to stay alert and your body cleansed. Second is complex sugar in which the molecules break down slowly, giving you steady energy. This is the reason why, if you go to a Chinese restaurant and stuff yourself on rice and vegetables, you may walk out thinking to yourself, 'I feel I didn't eat.'

Think of the relationship between food and stress. We often deal with stress by eating those foods which give us the reaction we need. If we want to eliminate feelings of depression, then sugar will stimulate us by creating a quick upper reaction. Correspondingly, if we are experiencing too much stress and we want to relax, then downer-type foods pacify us, causing us to feel tranquilized. We need to understand the relationship between stress addictions and success.

Television is also a downer. Watching the same station for just 30 seconds significantly reduces the electrical brain wave level frequencies, causing your mind to become mesmerized, often for hours. Research, though not well documented, indicates that television may cause atrophy of the dendrites on the brain cells. Television may also be the most passive activity.

Oversleep is a downer. Any adult who sleeps more than seven or eight hours per night is probably using sleep as an escape from reality. By purposefully oversleeping we avoid responsibilities that we do not want to confront.

Drugs can be both uppers and downers. Cocaine, LSD, psychedelic drugs and amphetamines are stimulants. Downers would be such tranquilizers as Valium, barbiturates and marijuana. Therefore, the type of drug which a person might become addicted to is a reflection of the cause of their frustration. A person who is addicted to uppers is someone who usually becomes bored easily and feels a need to be stimulated. If someone depends on downers, then they are probably having difficulty with reality, experiencing too much stress and wanting to tranquilize themselves.

Gambling and spending money would be an upper. Depression sets in later, when you run out of money.

Depression is a downer. Some people have a conditioned reaction to internalize stress. This manifests itself in such withdrawal and avoidance behavior as procrastination, lethargy and crying.

People who have a conditioned reaction to externalize stress can become violent and abusive. Starting arguments, irritating people just for the fun of it and hostility would be uppers.

Depending on uppers indicates that you hate boredom and enjoy being on the edge of disaster because it causes an adrenal high. Depending on downers indicates that your expectations are motivating you into situations which are so stressful that you seek devices to pacify your ego to emotionally survive.

Think of the extent to which you depend on these negative addictions and how this dependency affects your self-image.

In other words, what reflection is it of your self-image if you still depend on negative addictions? Obviously, you do not think very highly of yourself. The more positive your self-image, the more you are willing to suffer emotional pain and cravings to drop negatives and add positives.

The Positive Addictions

The first positive addiction is exercise, particularly an aerobic sport such as jogging, swimming, cycling, brisk walking, rowing, canoeing, aerobic dancing, cross-country skiing or snowshoeing. Convert the anxiety, which is energy, into an activity which gives you a sense of achievement. Gradually begin an exercise program after undergoing a doctor's checkup, as well as a stress test. Be easy on yourself as you increase your effort.

Stress is not a killer, only the reactions to stress. Also, the first symptom of a heart attack, in 26 percent of cases, is instant death. Obviously, this does not give the person much time to change the way he or she deals with stress. The most important foundation of our lives is our physical well-being. Only by being in good physical condition can we enjoy the success of our work and the relationships with our loved ones.

The second positive addiction is work. Take your work home with you. Then, if you become irritable, get some work done. The job is not using you. Rather, you are using the job to attain a sense of achievement.

The third positive addiction is relationships. Ask your employer for advice, brainstorm with an associate or counsel with a friend. Express your frustrations to a neighbor and enjoy quality time with loved ones. Play out feelings with someone you are close to.

The fourth positive addiction is solitude—in other words, being alone. More specifically, read a book, watch a sunset, play a musical instrument, engage in meditation or become spiritual.

You can become addicted to a positive activity as easily as to a negative one. All you need is ego-strength to make the transfer from one to the other.

Three Decisions

In conclusion, you need to make three decisions regarding these subjects of failure, rejection and anxiety. First, if ever again your life is not all you hoped it would be, then decide what you have gained. Remember *the benefits of failure.* Failure might not be as much fun as success, but it offers you many more benefits. Remember Buzz Aldrin, who landed on the moon. Afterward, he openly discussed the cause of his frustrations: "When you have landed on the moon, what else is there? What is the next challenge or the next amusement?" He could find nothing equally exciting. You want to continue to evolve and renew the adventure of reaching new levels of success. However, when you confront adversity, capitalize on the situation.

The second decision regards rejection. What could you do today to develop charismatic balance? How could you create, as in the martial arts of jujitsu, the ability to *react nicely* and be aggressively sensitive? Confrontation is part of our lives. People often become resistant and unreceptive of us. Most people avoid confrontation. Instead, to us some people will overreact and become hostile. React, but nicely. Rebound in a caring, sensitive way.

The third and last decision regards anxiety. Look at the list of negative addictions. Which one will you eliminate and which of the four positive addictions will you add or increase? If you discontinue a negative, but you do not add a positive, you might find yourself gaining weight or becoming irritable. When you eliminate a negative, you have to either add or increase a positive to absorb, relieve and channel the anxiety into productive activities which can assure your success.

Realize that, regarding your positive and negative addictions, you can feel good now and bad later, or bad now and good later. In other words, smoking or depending on alcohol or drugs to handle stress can make you feel just as you want to feel. Afterward, however, you might feel very bad. The hangover the next morning, or cirrhosis or lung cancer, is the result of your desire to feel good now without concern for the problems that you may experience in the future.

Instead, drop a negative and add a positive addiction. By doing so, you might feel bad now. A person who stops smoking usually will experience severe cravings. He or she may even feel worse by beginning an exercise program, particularly if the individual is not in shape. If you stay consistent and persevere, however, eventually the cravings for the negative addiction will disappear and you will *become addicted to the positive experience.* For example, the first quarter mile of jogging might be painful, but soon running a few miles might be easy.

Understand that the relationship between your success in selling, as well as in any part of your life, is directly related to your ability to capitalize on failure and rejection. Yet, failure and rejection are not so much the problem as the frustration and anxiety which these experiences create.

In conclusion, your ability to deal with stress has a direct relationship with your ability to succeed in selling or in any risk-oriented challenge.

For example, if someone gives you a selling technique, and the thought of trying an aggressive approach triggers stress until you are uncomfortable, then you may never achieve your own expectations.

If you were to thrive on anxiety, however, then stressful situations would create energy which would stimulate you to increase your effort.

Remember, an acorn becomes an oak tree by nature, but you become the person you were designed to be, not just by the courage to admit your frailties, but by the willingness to suffer through frustration and stress.

First, reevaluate your attitude toward failure. Think about your perception of reality. Understand your own expectations. Change your reactions.

Second, if a person is hostile to you, do not back off or overreact. Instead, react pleasantly until the person relaxes and becomes receptive to your suggestions.

Third, eliminate a negative addiction and add a positive. Make this change, not just to live longer and feel better, but for your own self-respect.

Remember this, from a man who understood that winning and losing is not our concern, but only our ability to capitalize on whatever occurs to us, Theodore Roosevelt: "Far better it is, to dare mighty things, to win glorious triumphs, even though checkered with failure, than to take rank with those poor spirits, who neither enjoy much, nor suffer much, because they live in the gray twilight that knows neither victory nor defeat."

PART
2

Mastering the Persuasion Process

4

The Stages of the Persuasion Process

*The buying decision is not a single decision
but a series of decisions.*

A rabbi, a priest and a minister went fishing each Monday. Then the minister was transferred and the priest and rabbi decided to invite the new minister for their weekly trip.

While fishing, the rabbi cast out his line. It tangled with the priest's line and the rabbi said, "Father, that was my fault. I'll take care of it." He then got out of the boat, tiptoed across the water, reached down and untangled the line. The minister, though shocked, attempted to keep his composure, acting as though it were perfectly normal to walk on water.

Later the priest cast his line and it became tangled in the minister's line. The priest said, "Pastor, that was my fault," stepped out of the boat, walked across the water, untangled the line and walked back. Again, the minister succeeded in keeping his composure.

Soon afterward, the minister tangled his line with that of the priest. With great apprehension, he said, "Father, that was my fault," stepped out of the boat and sank straight down. The rabbi turned to the priest and said, "Father, maybe we should show him where the rocks are."

This is our challenge when selling people on our ideas. We need to understand the steps we have to take, from where we are to where we need to be.

Think of the steps of persuasion, whether in selling, managing people or raising children.

AIDA THEORY

The original idea in selling is referred to as the AIDA theory:

- Attention,
- Interest,
- Desire and
- Action.

The first stage is attention, which is temporary and must be sustained long enough to gain the prospect's interest. Usually, attention can be gained by a well-phrased statement which will appeal to almost any prospect. During most cold calls, the prospect is unreceptive and will allow the salesperson only enough time to present one idea. For this reason, an attention-getting phase must be effective immediately. The salesperson then develops the interest into the kind of desire that culminates in action.

Thus, get the person's attention, develop their interest, create a desire, and then gain action, of the person buying your product.

As the years passed, few changes were made to the original theory. For example, during the 1930s, the word "conviction" was added, which was included in the Dale Carnegie Sales Training Program.

This original idea of selling was appropriate for the times. When selling simple products, a simple approach can be effective.

Think of selling a product such as a Model T Ford or a radio in the early twentieth century. Getting a person's attention is easy. Developing their interest can be automatic. Desire can occur spontaneously. Action often will follow quickly.

The types of products which many people sell today, however, are very complex. We are selling ideas and concepts which frequently are intangible and difficult to quantify.

The AIDA theory is obsolete, just as the Model T Ford. Of course, the Model T will take you where you want to go and it can be fun to watch. The concept of attention, interest, desire and action also can take you where you want to go, but there are more effective ways to travel to your destination.

The 1950s were a time of rapid change. Two world wars and the Depression were over, and new products, such as televisions and computers, were radically changing the way we lived and worked.

NEED-SATISFACTION THEORY

The effort to market more complex products and services demanded a more sophisticated philosophy of selling. This was accomplished using the need-satisfaction theory.

Determining Needs

We begin with the prospect's needs. We want to understand their concerns and objectives.

In other words, when selling simple products, we may only have to show the person how it operates and they will say, "That's exciting!" Yet a person's desires originate from their needs. When a prospect knows what they want, then the salesperson can more easily create a desire for the product. When the product is more complex, the prospect may not understand their needs and therefore may feel no desire for what we are offering.

As marketing people, we are taught to qualify prospects before we can create an interest and desire for what we are selling. From this single idea comes a series of important thoughts, such as counseling the prospect, developing questioning techniques for probing and conducting research to determine the prospect's applications.

Regardless of the familiarity that most salespeople have regarding the objective of determining needs, one aspect often is neglected, which is "need agreement."

Merely because we have determined the prospect's needs does not give us the right to assume that the prospect is equally familiar with their own requirements. In fact, the more complex the product we are selling, the less likely the prospect will be aware of their own needs.

As we become more sophisticated in marketing our services, we will benefit from the strategies and techniques used in the various fields of psychology, such as *counseling,* from which the Need-Satisfaction theory originates. In this approach, we realize that the prospect often may be frustrated, because of unsatisfied needs or unresolved problems, yet still be unaware of what their actual needs or problems might be.

For example, during more than 20 years of giving lectures, I would write the names of my prospective clients and steady customers on yellow pads or index cards. Frequently, I would lose or misplace the names of people I needed to contact or become confused by my own handwritten notes.

My older son, after finishing college, joined my business and recommended purchasing a computer and a laser printer. I told him that while I was frustrated by my prospecting system, I felt no need to spend money on the equipment, even with the added benefits of text and letter writing and other record-keeping systems.

He persevered pleasantly, using a variety of my techniques, until I reluctantly agreed to his suggestions. Now I cannot imagine functioning without this simple system.

Every business conversation ends with the question, "...and when should I call you back?" If I am calling to thank the person for coordinating a presentation I recently gave, I will finish the discussion with "...and when should I call back to discuss my presenting the second part?"

Then I type the names of my clients into the computer, by name, telephone number and date to call back, with any unique details. Next, the laser printer sorts more than a thousand names by the follow-up date and allows me to control my lecture schedule. Equally, the development of this new book is more efficient, as well as accounting, letter writing and handling a variety of records.

Being frustrated by unsatisfied needs did not cause me to be aware of my requirements. This is why salespeople have to help prospects become aware of their problems, even when they are operating inefficiently. Only then can we present our recommendations for their consideration.

Before we can present our recommendations, we must gain the prospects' agreement of what their needs might be. In psychology, and more specifically in counseling, we first ask questions and then listen. Becoming sophisticated in selling, therefore, requires becoming a better listener. We need to emphasize asking questions and really listening to the prospect if we are to understand their concerns and frustrations.

The classic method of determining the prospect's needs is by asking questions, particularly open-ended questions. Such questions cannot be answered positively or negatively, but only by expressing an opinion. For example, "How do you feel about life insurance?", "What do you feel is the best investment during these unusual times?" or "What are your views on computer applications within your company?"

Consider the benefits of an open-ended question:

- You gain insight into the prospect's needs and problems;
- You better understand their personality and what is important to them;
- You cause prospects to feel that you are concerned about them as you listen to their feelings;
- You can decide where agreement exists, as well as disagreement and possible conflict; and
- You have time to think of what you want to say next.

Direct questions are used when there is value in gaining a yes or no response, such as when you make a suggestion and finish by asking, "Does this make sense to you?" You frequently need to know if the prospect's thinking is in a red- or green-light mode.

There is, however, a danger in asking questions. People feel that the information which they present might be used against them. For example, if a prospect admits that he or she has no life insurance, then he or she is concerned that the agent may become very persistent. For this reason, there are more subtle ways to determine the prospect's thoughts and feelings.

The Art of Being Interrupted

Think of those times when you have been at a social gathering and a group of five or six people are conversing. Notice that usually one person often controls the conversation and others may have difficulty interrupting this person. Then there are some people who, whenever they begin speaking, cannot seem to finish a sentence without someone interrupting.

Also, realize when you ask people questions, particularly in a selling environment, they usually will assume that your purpose is to sell them your product. Even a question which you ask to establish rapport, such as asking about their family or favorite sport, can irritate a prospect when he or she believes that your only purpose is to increase their receptivity.

Yet if you were to speak in such a way that the prospect were to interrupt you and finish your sentence for you, then you might be intrigued by the insight you gain into their true thoughts and feelings. Ask a question and you often may receive a dishonest or misleading answer, for the person avoids disclosing information which they are afraid you may use against them. Allow the person to interrupt you and the spontaneous reaction invariably will be an honest one.

Consider why people have interrupted you. Though frustrating, you have to admit that you were observing the person's real thoughts and feelings. If you give some thought to the way you verbalize your ideas, particularly the way in which you pause and the inflection of your voice, you may realize that you actually are encouraging people to interrupt you.

Since your objective is to gain insight into the prospect's needs, desires and attitudes, you want to be interrupted. Your approach is to begin speaking without being specific and pause frequently, particularly in the middle of a sentence. For example, "I don't know what your feelings are on investing,...but it is interesting to realize what a small percentage of our population is financially independent at the age of sixty-five,...particularly when you think of the various ways to invest...and I don't know what your opinion is...of the approach to use...to provide for the future..."

With certain inflections and properly placed pauses, people will be interrupting you and finishing your sentences. Since people never would suspect you wanted to be interrupted, their spontaneous response will give you insight into their inner feelings.

Your success in marketing complex ideas, therefore, may require reevaluating your image of yourself, as well as your perception of your responsibilities, and beginning to see yourself as a counselor. Before trying to create a desire for your ideas, you first determine the prospect's needs and do not attempt to solve problems until you know what is frustrating the prospect. You also gain agreement that the prospect needs to change, before you offer your recommendations.

In review, the first objective, to understand the prospect's needs, is a two-part process:

- Determining a prospect's needs and
- Gaining agreement of what his or her needs may be.

Once you have determined the prospect's needs and he or she agrees that certain changes must be made, then you are ready to strive for his or her satisfaction.

Gaining Satisfaction

The second objective in this theory is to gain the prospect's *satisfaction*. The word has two parts—*satisfy* and *action*.

First, you want to satisfy prospective customers by doing what is right for them. You also want to gain action, in which you make the sale and achieve your own sales objectives. Generally, there are two types of salespeople: those who want to satisfy people and those who want action.

If you are people-oriented, then your primary objective probably will be to please the prospect; therefore, you will be "satisfy"-oriented.

If your primary goal is to make money by getting the sale, then you most likely will be "action"-oriented.

If you want to satisfy people, but are not action-oriented, however, you may develop many good prospects, but achieve little success in your marketing objectives. Correspondingly, if you are action-oriented, then you would be returning to the old theory of AIDA and, while often making the quick sale, might not satisfy your customers. Thus, you may lose long-term results. More specifically, you may have difficulty gaining repeat business, marketing diversified products and developing referrals, and find yourself in a continuous "numbers game."

The successful salesperson strives to achieve both objectives, to satisfy people and gain action. Thus, successful salespeople usually develop long-term relationships and consistent results.

An inherent conflict exists between gaining immediate results and developing long-term relationships. If you are selling simple products, such as vacuum cleaners or magazine subscriptions, your success requires some rapport but considerable ability to create excitement about your product, to resolve objections and to close.

If you are marketing computer equipment, which may require the prospect's investment of a sizable amount of money, you may have to develop considerable rapport and an awareness of the prospect's requirement during a period of a year or more before attempting to gain results.

Many products, however, require a somewhat equal balance between establishing the relationship and pursuing the results. These products include financial services such as stocks and bonds and small computer systems.

Many corporations, in becoming market-driven, are teaching their sales training force to focus on customer satisfaction and seek long-term relationships. Then, when these salespeople return to their branch offices, they often are told by their managers to disregard what they were taught and concentrate on immediate results.

One illustration of this potential conflict occurred when a bank trained its tellers to sell diversified products such as traveler's checks. When the tellers returned to their jobs, they would ask customers, while processing their transactions, when they were planning their vacations and if they would need traveler's checks, which the bank could provide. The branch managers then became upset because the conversation caused the lines to move slowly and the customers to become impatient.

In review, if you have a headache and the doctor suggests taking aspirin and the pain goes away, then the simple solution has resolved a simple problem. When the needs become more complex, however, such as the processing of data and information in a major corporation, the analysis of the prospect's computer requirements becomes a more intricate process.

We need to use good judgment to create the necessary balance between these two objectives, of satisfy/relationships and action/results. Consider the following guidelines:

- Contact as many prospects, as quickly as possible, to determine who has an immediate need and therefore represents the opportunity for quick sales.
- Use a selling approach that creates receptivity, so you can follow up and develop a long-term relationship.
- Strive to gain immediate business, while devoting part of your day to developing long-term relationships.

If you enjoy the challenge of persuading people to your way of thinking, which is action-oriented, and if you also like to help people, which is satisfy-oriented, then you have to balance a number of factors:

1. The complexity of the products or services which you are marketing:

- the less complex, the more you can seek action;
- the more complex, the more you must satisfy.
2. The prospect's awareness of or lack of familiarity with their requirements:
   - the more aware, the more you can move quickly;
   - the less aware, the more you need to get involved.
3. Your ability to employ various techniques to determine the prospect's situation:
   - the more quickly you can understand a prospect's needs, the more quickly you can seek results;
   - the more difficult the process of determining a prospect's requirements, the more patient you need to be.
4. Your ability to gain the prospect's agreement that there is a need to change:
   - the more effective you might be in persuading the prospect that they have a problem which needs to be resolved, the sooner you can move on to the close;
   - the less receptive the prospect might be, regarding their need to make a change, the more you must calmly persevere through this process.

Yet if you are sensitive to the prospect's position and coordinate your approach with their thinking process, you will eliminate objections before they occur. The only moments during which objections may concern you, therefore, is when presenting solutions.

One way to resolve objections is to anticipate them. If you understand the prospect's concern, then you may correctly assume what potential disagreement might exist. If you address the prospect's concerns within the presentation of your product, you might resolve the objections before the prospect becomes concerned.

Many salespeople are trained to disregard objections. If the prospect expresses negative feelings, the salesperson is instructed to continue the presentation and act as though no problem exists. This approach might be valid if:

- The product is simple;
- The need is obvious;
- The prospecting objections are minor; and
- The salesperson is ego-centered and desires to satisfy only their own needs.

The more sensitive you become regarding the prospect's needs and the results you will gain, the more you will want to understand the prospect's concerns and resolve any objections.

SERIES OF DECISIONS THEORY

During the same time that the Need-Satisfaction theory was being developed, we also became acquainted with a theory that is more advanced, but still relatively unknown. This is the Series of Decisions theory which states that *the buying decision is not a single decision, but a series of decisions.*

This theory is the most customer-oriented selling approach available. This strategy places you on the customer's side of the table and brings you into their thinking process. It is symbolic of a market-driven strategy.

We need to realize that when we think in terms of selling, we are being egocentric, such as when we were children and believed that the world revolved around us. If we are to center on the prospect, then we no longer think in terms of selling, of what we are trying to achieve, but in the decisions the prospect is making, of what is important to them.

As an illustration, think of a product you purchased, such as a car. If you love your car, then you proudly will tell people, "Look what I bought." If you do not like you car, however, you will tell people, "Look at the lemon I was sold."

People do not want to be sold, they want to buy.

If you sell them, they may question the value of the product and may begin to feel they were forced to buy or that in some way they were manipulated into the purchase.

If they decide that they bought the product, however, then there is a greater likelihood that they will be happy with their decision. The chance of buyer's remorse is reduced significantly, and the opportunities for repeat business, referrals and discovering additional applications are increased.

Therefore, if you imagine yourself in the mind of the prospect, and begin to think as they do, then you will understand the decisions that need to be made, including the actual buying decision.

More specifically, one of your primary business objectives today is being market-driven. The major success of the Japanese might be their ability to focus on the "hot buttons" of the market. They think of what people want. They put themselves in the buyer's position. They concentrate on what motivates the consumer.

As a personal example, I enjoy playing chess. My friend was leading five games to two. Most upsetting was that I suspected my two victories had occurred because I was so far behind that he became bored and lost his concentration.

In the next game, he was winning again when, in increased desperation, I stood up and walked behind him. From his side of the table, I could see clearly what he was doing and that he was not so brilliant as I had been assuming, but rather that I had been intellectually blind. I then won that game, and the next four, and presently have a seven-to-five lead.

Developing an effective game plan requires understanding the prospect's strategy. You need to think as the prospect does. You need to see yourself and your products as the prospect does. You need to disengage your ego and feel the way the prospect feels. Think of the decisions, therefore, which the prospect needs to make to hopefully culminate in the buying decision and their satisfaction.

"Do I Want To See This Person?"

The first decision usually is, "Do I want to see this person?" In other words, when the secretary or assistant notifies the prospect that you are on the telephone or at the door, the prospect may ask, "Do I want to sacrifice any of my time for this salesperson?" If the decision is negative, then the conversation has ended before you had a chance to begin.

In this approach to selling, therefore, your first concern is to think as the prospect is thinking and decide what method or words to use so the prospect will want to meet with you.

"Do I Want To Talk to You?"

If the prospect decides to see you, then your next challenge is to gain a positive response to their second decision, "Do I want to talk to you?"

You cannot assume, merely because the prospect agrees to see you, that they will listen to you. More specifically, as you begin speaking with the prospect, he or she may conclude, "I am not interested in what this salesperson has to say," and end the conversation.

For this reason, you need to be very sensitive to the prospect's attention span. Just as children can concentrate on the same subject for only a certain time, and then become bored and even irritable, the prospect also may become disinterested.

Of course, the child might become fascinated with a television program or a bedtime story and might not want to be interrupted. This, equally, is your challenge in selling. You want to stimulate the prospect's thinking to gain the necessary attention span.

When I sold for IBM, I would imagine that, once the prospect invited me into their office, it was as though a candle was lit. Now the challenge was to keep the candle burning for as long as possible, or until I had achieved my initial objective, which was to gain some form of agreement, such as making a presentation.

One of my most satisfying experiences was when the prospect would tell me that he or she was not interested, but would at least give me a few minutes. When I sat down with the prospect, I would try to be very sensitive of how much time I had to convert their attention into interest. I would try to stimulate the prospect's thinking so they would decide, "This is very interesting," and give me enough time to achieve my immediate objective, such as determining their needs.

I merged the AIDA and the Series of Decisions theories to gain a more meaningful understanding of what I needed to accomplish. It was as though I were operating a computer and attempting to find those hot buttons which would give me the reaction I needed, so that the prospect would become interested in what I was selling.

With these thoughts in mind, think of the prospect's next decision. He or she has decided, "Yes, I will see you." and "Yes, I do feel that what you have to say is worth listening to." Now consider what the prospect's third decision might be.

"Do I Have a Need?"

Often a person may become excited about a product and therefore become responsive to you, but have no need for what you are selling. Of course, certain salespeople frequently make the sale, though the prospect has no need for the product, because of the salesperson's ability to create a desire. This is referred to as impulse buying. In other words, we are selling on emotions rather than on need. How often have you heard someone say, "Why did you buy that when you had no need for it?"

Why would someone spend extra money on a car because it can go from zero to 100 miles per hour in x seconds, when 55 or 65 is the maximum speed limit? We often spend considerable money on products that satisfy needs which are more psychological in origin, such as ego needs to feel important, rather than functional or practical needs.

Successful salespeople, therefore, often are not selling the product, but what the product can do for the customer. If the product has no practical purpose, then the selling message usually will be designed to appeal to an ego need, which is playing on our emotions.

Consider cigarette advertising. We see a young couple in a rowboat in a beautiful setting. The cigarette may not be shown and the smoking might not even be noticeable. The message is to convince young people that if they smoke that brand, they will be considered an adult and will enjoy a romantic life.

When you watch the beer advertisement, you see "macho" men gathering together in a male-bonding environment. The advertiser is trying to convince the viewer that if he drinks this beer, he will be masculine and his friends will accept him as "one of the guys."

In the advertisement for an expensive sedan, we see a mansion in the background, which is different from the advertisement for a red sports car showing a young couple having a picnic in a secluded place. Thus, we often are buying a car which is a reflection of our self-image or, more importantly, the image we wish to have of ourselves or to portray to others. The product, therefore, is not designed to satisfy functional needs as much as satisfying psychological needs, such as to impress others and to gain peer-group acceptance.

The design of some cars is considered a phallic symbol and that by buying the car, a man may resolve problems of his own insecurity. We also are aware of how some women want a strong man to make them feel secure, and the man therefore will buy a car that symbolizes power. He senses that "power is the ultimate aphrodisiac."

Yet some consumers who are motivated emotionally by psychological needs still need to justify the purchase by convincing themselves that they are buying for practical purposes. The salesperson, therefore, might use two messages: one to appeal to ego-emotional-status needs and the other to justify the purchase.

In marketing, we need to recognize the diversity of our culture. We have a strong puritanical background that requires that we be sensible, work hard and save our money. Equally, we live in a society which is materialistic, status-oriented and pleasure-seeking. Thus, products are diversified to satisfy the various segments of the market. This is referred to as *product diversification for market segmentation.* In other words, we diversify our products so as to satisfy each segment of the market.

Correspondingly, our selling strategy and persuasive techniques must relate to what motivates the prospect. We need to illustrate those features which will satisfy the buyer within the spectrum of both their ego—emotional—needs and their practical—objective—needs.

Beyond Emotional and Practical Needs

Our society is evolving so rapidly that we often find ourselves in the middle of changes which are difficult to understand. It is not easy to recognize the forces which surround us when we are in the middle of a storm.

Consider the need to communicate more quickly and efficiently, thus the demand for cellular phones, video conferencing and fax machines. What was once considered futuristic, and then a fad, now is a necessity. Marketing strategy often focuses on needs that are neither practical nor ego-oriented, but might be more appropriately referred to as sophisticated.

The need to increase the availability of information to quicken the decision-making process, with a reduced risk of error, sharpens the demand for computer technology—thus, the rapid development of more sophisticated equipment and software and the corresponding demand for a selling approach which corresponds to the complex needs of the consumer.

Therefore, when we evolve from the

- AIDA theory, of creating a desire for products in which the prospect's needs often are obvious, to the

- Need-Satisfaction theory, in which we attempt to satisfy more complex needs, of which the prospect might not even be familiar, to the
- Series of Decisions theory, in which we are selling sophisticated products, we need to understand what is meant by being market-driven.

The challenge to the marketer is to see the world from the prospects' viewpoints, to think as they think, feel as they feel and listen to the questions they are asking, such as, "Are you correct in your analysis of my needs that I do have a problem?" Only then can we understand how to gain more than an immediate sale but to create the kind of relationship which culminates in repeat business, the satisfying of complex needs with diversified products and, therefore, the assurance of our eventual success.

The prospect's third decision is, "Do I have a need?" or "Are you correct in believing that I have a problem?"

"Do You Have What I Need?"

The next decision, assuming the prospect decides that they have a need, is when the prospect asks, "Does this person have what I need?" or "Does this salesperson have the solutions to my problems?"

Just because you may have succeeded in developing or sharpening the prospect's awareness of their situation, do not assume that they will buy your product. Often, unfortunately, your selling skills may only cause the person to decide that, if he or she does make a change, it may be to a competitive product. This could occur because the competitor is more prestigious, the product less expensive or more familiar or, possibly, the prospect has a personal relationship with the salesperson.

You cannot assume, therefore, that just because you have "created the need" or made the prospect aware of their requirements, that the sale automatically will follow. In fact, all that you may have accomplished is to help a competitor, who may have failed to generate need awareness, to get the order.

Yet throughout this process is an even more basic concern regarding the prospect's needs. You may succeed in creating need-awareness, but the prospect may have other objectives which cause their priorities to relegate your product to a secondary position.

If this occurs, you have choices. You can accept the prospect's decision and ask when you may call again, that the prospect's priorities may have changed and that he or she may be interested.

"Do I Have a Problem?"

However, if you sincerely believe that the prospect is disregarding a need that, if not satisfied, could become a problem, then your challenge is to make the prospect aware of the severity of their situation.

This is one of the most overlooked and crucial stages of the persuasion process. Realize that many people change only when they have no other choice. Most people would rather "stay in the frying pan" than change and take a chance on "jumping into the fire."

Think of the reasons most people would remain in a negative or less-desirable situation rather than change:

- Some people are reluctant to change because of bad experiences.
- Possibly they feel a loyalty to their existing salesperson.
- Maybe they feel insecure regarding unfamiliar situations.
- They may lack the information required to make an intelligent decision.

Regardless of their reluctance, you may have no choice but to describe reality. In other words, you need to make them aware that a crisis will exist if they do not make a change.

In the movie and play *Music Man*, Robert Preston sang a song, "Trouble in River City." He disturbed the townspeople when he told them that their boys were down at the pool hall, had nicotine stains on their fingers and were using the word "swell." When he was finished telling them of the trouble in their city, everyone bought his musical instruments for a boys' band.

Often, in selling, we simplify the process into just two steps:

- Problem awareness and
- Solution presentation.

In this process, we temporarily postpone presenting solutions and focus on creating an awareness of the problem. If we are successful in causing the prospect to become concerned of the crisis he or she is in, then the prospect will be asking us for solutions.

For example, the computer salesperson may explain to the decision maker, "I've met with your department executives. Do you know how frustrated your information services manager is? Are you aware of what your competitor is doing with new computer applications? Are you familiar with the relationship between rising costs and the solutions offered by advanced computer technology? Do you know the problems you are having in inventory control and truck routing?" Suddenly, the prospect is interrupting the salesperson, saying, "I was not aware of how much trouble I was in. Can you possibly help me?" The response: "Of course I can."

Avoid presenting solutions to a prospect until he or she is familiar with the nature of their problem. Then the prospect will ask if you can help, which is the ideal situation. At least, the prospect might be more receptive when you suggest ways you can help. You want to gain a positive response to the prospect's question, "If I do not change, is this salesperson correct, that I may then be in serious trouble?"

"Is This the Solution?"

If the prospect decides, "I have a need" or "I have a problem," then move to the next question within this Series of Decisions, which is: "Does this salesperson have the solution for me?"

As discussed previously, you might be successful in selling the prospect on the idea that he or she has a need to be satisfied or a problem to be solved, but the prospect may decide to buy from someone else.

Even more so, the prospect may agree that you have the solutions to the problem, but still have objections. In other words, agreement or disagreement is not always black or white but varying degrees of gray. The prospect, for example, may want to buy, but be confused by one aspect of your product and may not want to reveal what is distracting. The prospect needs to make a decision, therefore, as expressed in the question, "Do I really believe I need this product?" or "Do I really understand how this product is going to benefit me?"

For those of us in selling, we have to wonder how often we have come so close to gaining agreement and yet have not succeeded because of an objection we did not resolve.

"Has This Salesperson Resolved My Objections?"

Throughout the selling process, you may confront objections. For example, if you ask for too much, the prospect may become frustrated. If you ask to speak to the prospect when they are distracted by other priorities or they are in a crisis, then you may only increase their frustrations. If you speak beyond the prospect's attention span and degree of interest, you may only anger them. If you assume that the prospect understands their needs, which is different than what the prospect perceives, you may only antagonize the person. If you present solutions before the prospect feels that they have a need, you may cause the prospect to assume that you are trying to sell only for your benefit.

"Is the Price Right?"

More specifically, prospects often decide that they want the product, but are concerned about the cost. Thus, they might ask themselves, "Is the price right?"

You may, therefore, succeed in gaining a positive decision to the question, "Will this product solve my problem?", but the prospect may not be able to justify the cost.

If you know that the prospect is in this stage of the decision-making process, however, you might be able to resolve their concern. Maybe you could offer a payment plan, discuss tax benefits or illustrate an increase in productivity.

"Is the Time Right?"

Correspondingly, you may justify the price, but then the prospect may ask, "Is the time right?"

Often the prospect may have just made an investment and, while he or she may prefer your product and feel the cost is reasonable, the prospect may not need what you are offering for a given time period.

"Am I Satisfied with the Product?"

Even when you gain the buying decision, you must remember that a sale does not end with the sale but with the customer's satisfaction. You have to put yourself in the other person's position and answer the question in their mind, "Am I satisfied with the product?"

If the response is not positive, then you might be disappointed when confronting buyer's remorse or dealing with a cancellation.

The more sensitive you are regarding customer satisfaction, the more responsive you can be when following up and assuring that he or she is pleased. In this way, you may resolve buyer's remorse before it occurs, gain referrals and repeat business, as well as explore other applications as a way of marketing other products.

In review, think of the questions within the prospect's "Series of Decisions":

- Do I want to see this salesperson?
- Do I want to listen to this person?
- Is this someone I can trust?
- Is this a person I can depend on?
- Do I really have a need?
- Do I have a problem and, therefore, a need to make a change?
- Will this salesperson's solutions resolve my problems?
- Has this person resolved my objections?
- Is the price right?
- Is the time right?
- Should I sign now?
- Am I satisfied?

You need to answer each question to move easily to the prospect's next decision, so prepare for these questions, using each of your responses as a separate module or game plan. Otherwise, you may confront resistance which will prevent you from moving to the next stage of this process. Too often, prospects do not express resistance. Instead, they hide their frustrations with smoke-screen objections. If they feel the price is too high, for example, they may instead tell you the time is not right.

Now consider the Series of Decisions theory within the challenge of managing resistance. Convert each decision into varying forms and degrees of resistance:

- I have no desire to see or listen to this salesperson.
- I do not like this salesperson.
- I do not feel I can trust this salesperson.

- I do not feel I can depend on this salesperson.
- I do not believe I have any need to change.
- While I have decided to make a change, I do not believe this salesperson's product is what I want.
- I am interested in buying the product, but this salesperson is not resolving my objections.
- While I want to buy the product, the price is too high.
- While the price is right, this is not the time for me to make such a purchase.
- Now that I have bought the product, I am concerned that I may have made a mistake.

If you transform each of these negative thoughts into a challenge, then you may feel stimulated to move through each as a passageway to eventual customer satisfaction. Enjoy converting each level of resistance into stepping-stones toward your desired objective by deciding what you will say to resolve each of these various forms of resistance.

In review, the challenge is a four-step process of:

1. Recognizing and disengaging the prospect's *resistance.*
2. Gaining the prospect's *receptivity.*
3. Developing an ideal *relationship.*
4. Achieving the *desired results.*

Think of the way you react when considering the possibility of defeat. If the fear of failing or being rejected causes you to become defensive, then such thinking is dangerous. Yet think of how the same mental process can work for your benefit.

For example, consider why you may fail in your present job. You may wonder why such a negative thought is being presented. However, if you were taking a vacation in the Caribbean in September or skiing in the Rocky Mountains in January, you first would review the weather report. You would not want to find yourself in the middle of a storm and wonder how you got yourself into so much trouble.

Equally, when taking on a challenge, you want to forecast any potential problems. Therefore, if the storm begins, you are prepared.

Correspondingly, in contacting a prospect, you need to anticipate the prospect's reaction, even if this reaction might be negative. Then develop a game plan which will deal effectively with each possible storm of resistance.

5

Relationships and Results

The depth of the rapport determines the sensitivity of the issue.

DEVELOPING THE RELATIONSHIP

As salespeople, we have two primary responsibilities. The first is to develop good *relationships* with our prospects and customers. This requires achieving three objectives.

The first objective is establishing rapport, which requires the ability to relate to people. The more effectively you can relate to people, the more easily you will *develop rapport*.

Establishing rapport earns you the right to probe, ask questions and to *determine* the other person's *needs*, which is the second objective.

Imagine that you are in an elevator with a stranger. You probably would feel comfortable asking the person about the weather. You may, however, create a problem if you were to ask, "Sir, you don't look so good. You seem to have been drinking. Are there any personal problems you would like to discuss with me?"

The depth of the rapport determines the sensitivity of the issue. The more sensitive the subject you want to discuss, the greater the rapport must be. Asking a stranger a question regarding the weather is not serious, but asking someone about their personal problems usually requires a significant degree of rapport.

As an illustration, the youngest of my four children is now 23. Despite their ages, I still am aggressively concerned about them. I usually challenge at least one of them in some way each day. Frequently, my child reacts by saying, "No, Dad, I don't want to discuss this with you."

In that moment I realize that I have one of two problems. Either the issue I am attempting to discuss is far more sensitive for my child than I realized or the rapport is not as great as I thought it was. Correspondingly, I have two solutions. One is to *reduce the sensitivity of the issue.* In other words, I could say, "OK. Let's drop the subject; but could we at least discuss this one small part?" The other solution is to *increase the rapport.* For example, I may say, "OK, but how about dinner this weekend, just you and me; so I can at least tell you why I am so concerned."

Think of the complexity of what you are selling. If you sell magazine subscriptions over the telephone, then the subject is not sensitive and the required rapport is only minimal. An investment program, however, in which you need to know the prospect's tax bracket, what type of life insurance he or she presently has and how the prospect is investing their money, requires developing a significant degree of rapport.

Specifically, if a person ever says to you, "What right do you have to ask me that kind of question?", they actually are saying, "You have not earned the right to ask me." However, prospects who feel that you sincerely care about them will become relaxed and responsive with you.

People love to express their frustrations and talk about themselves, if they feel comfortable with the person in whom they are confiding. This becomes your challenge: to create the kind of rapport that causes the person to want to discuss their inner feelings. In this way, you gain insight into the prospect's needs and frustrations. Consider the sensitivity of the issues you wish to discuss with the prospect and how much rapport you therefore need to first establish.

You must be *understanding* when determining needs. Consider, for example, your personal life, such as a love relationship. Of what value is love without understanding? When you are in conflict with someone you love, and you understand why the person is behaving as he or she is, the understanding can cause your frustration to dissipate.

Once you understand the prospect's needs, then you can develop and *present solutions.* The primary quality required to achieve this third objective is your ability to help people.

In review,

relating to people allows you to establish the *rapport* necessary to *understand* their *needs,*
so you can *help* them with your *solutions.*

These are three steps to gaining an ideal relationship.

GAINING RESULTS

The second primary responsibility you have in selling is to gain results. You want to close the sale, reach your quota and make money. This requires achieving three objectives.

The first is *describing reality.* You may have established rapport and determined the prospect's needs, but he or she may not agree with you regarding what these needs might be. You cannot present solutions, therefore, until the prospect decides that he or she has a need to change.

In politics, for example, the challenger cannot replace the incumbent if people are comfortable with the present administration. Even if problems exist, and the majority of the public is frustrated, change still may not occur, for fear that change may only compound the problem. The challenger only will succeed if he or she can disturb the public regarding the severity of the situation and assure the voters that only through change will they become more comfortable.

This challenge obviously is a difficult task. For this reason, the vice president often replaces the existing president in the next election, because people feel comfortable with the status quo.

Once a person decides to change, either because you have gained their agreement regarding their needs or explained to the prospect the severity of their problems, then you are ready to present solutions. When presenting solutions, however, people often will voice objections which you must resolve. Thus, the second objective in gaining results is *overcoming objections.*

The third stage is *gaining agreement.* In selling, this last stage is referred to as the close.

Now consider the prospect's psychological needs which you must satisfy if you are to develop a good relationship and gain results.

Trust

Developing good relationships with prospects occurs when they decide that you are someone they can confide in and that your recommendations are for their benefit. If you want people to open up to you and believe in what you say, you must convince them that they can *trust* you.

Consider how important this single word might be. First think of how important relationships are in your life. Then realize that the quality of the relationship is only a by-product of the extent in which someone feels that he or she can trust you. The more someone trusts you, the greater the relationship.

Dependability

Correspondingly, consider what is required to gain results. If you want people to assume that you are an authority and accept your advice, then you must convince them that they can *depend* on you. If people are to feel comfortable following your instructions, then they need to respect you and rely on you. Think of how important results are in your life and that results are only a by-product of how much someone feels that he or she can depend on you.

"I Care about You"

Now for the next part of this process. People trust you when you assure them that "I care about you." Only when people feel you care about them will they trust you, so you can establish rapport and develop good relationships.

In the often-cited Western Electric Company study of 1927–32 at the Hawthorne Plant in Cicero, Illinois, the industrial psychologists wanted to determine the extent in which they could increase production by upgrading working conditions, so they improved the lighting and production increased. As they continued to improve lighting, production continued to rise. As a way of validating their study, the psychologists then reduced the lighting to discover to what extent production would decrease and were surprised to observe that production rose even higher.

The correct conclusion was that the workers felt that management was interested in them. They could see people observing them, people who seemed to be very concerned about them. The more attention they felt they were receiving, the more they believed that people cared about them.

When you meet someone for the first time, particularly in a selling situation, remember that the person is asking you, unconsciously and spontaneously, "Are you someone who cares about me?" *The more you assure people that you care about them, the more they will trust you, and thus the greater the relationship.*

"I Can Take Care of You"

What causes people to feel they can depend on you is when you assure them that "I can you take care of you."

If you want people to assume that you are an authority, whom they can rely on to resolve their problems, then you want to assure them that you can take care of them. Only then will they depend on you. Then you can achieve your objectives and gain the desired results.

Warm and Sensitive

If you want people to believe that you care about them, and therefore gain an ideal relationship, you need to project a certain type of personality. Think of the person who assures you that you can trust them—someone you can confide in and believe that whatever they say is for your benefit.

Such people are warm, sensitive, pleasant, caring, honest, sincere, kind, loving, compassionate, empathetic and friendly. Which two or three words do you believe symbolize the type of person who assures you that they care about you? In other words, think of the qualities of someone you can trust who causes you to feel comfortable in developing a close relationship.

Aggressive and Dominant

Now consider the type of person who assures you that they can take care of you, so you feel comfortable depending on them and following their recommendations. Such people, regardless of their inner personalities, project that they are confident, decisive, tough, forceful, resilient, persistent, dominant, reactive and aggressive.

Which two or three qualities would you select to represent a person who you respect, as someone you can rely on?

Two Behavioral Patterns

Thus, we have two types of personalities and behavioral patterns. In review, think of which of the two following patterns seem most like you:

- Are you a warm, sensitive person who convinces people that you care about them so they can trust you? If so, you easily will establish rapport, create good relationships and quickly develop prospects.

    If, however, for fear of rejection, you are not an aggressive, confident person, then people may not feel comfortable depending on you. For this reason, you frequently may wonder why, though developing good relationships and great prospects, you have so little results to justify your effort.

- Correspondingly, if you are an aggressive, decisive person who quickly establishes a position of authority, then people may decide they can depend on you to take care of them. Therefore, they will follow your instructions and you will gain good results.

    If, however, for fear of appearing weak, you are not warm and sensitive, then people may question your sincerity and feel they were "hustled." Your customers may experience buyer's remorse and you may receive cancellations. You also may find yourself in a continuous numbers game in which you have to attract new prospects and customers, because your avoidance of humility and warmth causes distrust, a lack of repeat business and attrition of clients.

Enhance Yourself

If you can develop the qualities of these two opposite personalities within the appropriate balance, then people will feel as though you care about them and also that you can take care of them. People will trust you and depend on you and you will create strong relationships with great results.

Now decide where change may occur. In other words, do you need to become more sensitive to establish better relationships or more decisive to gain results?

If you have yet to develop the perfect balance, then what change may be necessary? The process of creating balance does not require a personality change, but rather enhancing your self-image and the impression you create.

In other words, you cannot be too aggressive, for aggressiveness is a great quality. Aggressiveness, however, also can be obnoxious. If your aggressiveness becomes abrasive, then do not reduce this quality and avoid challenges. Rather, enhance your aggressiveness with sensitivity.

Equally, you cannot be too sensitive, for sensitivity is one of the most important personality qualities. Sensitivity by itself, however, can cause vulnerability. If you become too sensitive, then do not "chill out" or become cynical. Rather, enhance your sensitivity with confidence, resiliency and inner strength.

You can never be too much of a certain type of person. If you ever possess too much of a given quality, then do not reduce what you have and become less than what you are. Instead become more of a person by developing the opposite side. Enhance yourself. Become *aggressively sensitive.*

The Perfect Child

Watch children between the ages of one and four. They are perfect—for four reasons. Consider these four qualities and decide if you still possess each of these attributes.

Relentlessness

First, children are relentless. When they know what they want, they are eternally persistent.

Proficient Role Playing

Second, they are proficient role players. They know how to speak with you to obtain what they want, which often will be very different than the way they are with someone else; and they enjoy it. In other words, they enjoy being like a star on a Broadway show and being able to relate to everyone to always get what they want. If you think about this ability, you may agree that it makes sense to relate with everyone to always get what you want.

Agility at Shifting Gears

Third, children "shift gears at high speeds." In other words, if one approach does not work, then they move on to the next technique. More than relating to people, they are able to keep trying new techniques until they find one that gains agreement, such as the chocolate chip cookie they desire.

Think of these last two qualities and imagine you are making an improvement in your home, such as remodeling a room. You have received the names of two contractors to evaluate.

The first person is someone you automatically like. You feel an instant rapport with this person. When you ask a question, however, the person uses terminology you do not understand, and when you express an objection, their response is, "Don't worry about it."

The second person is just not your type of person. You do not dislike this person, but you do not relate to him or her. Yet when you ask a question, the person uses words which you easily understand, and whenever you voice an objection, you are given a thorough and sensible explanation.

Which person would you select? The primary thought is to illustrate that you need both. One without the other will leave you vulnerable to your competition and, in some varying form, a distraction to your prospective customers. The perfect child has both qualities.

Disarming

Last of all, you cannot be upset with children's relentless persistence, proficient role playing and high-speed shifting of gears because they are so cute! They are cheerful, amusing, friendly, witty, intelligent and brilliant.

Children, at three years of age, are *professional hustlers.*

Therefore, to be successful in selling does not require changing your personality: just return to the perfect child within you.

If you have forgotten how perfect you were at three, then watch children of that age. Most likely, you were as relentless and as charming as they are.

If you are not as perfect today as when you were three years old, then why have you lost some of your inner child's qualities? Maybe you can think back to a time when you were warm and sensitive and someone took advantage of your kindness or hurt your feelings. You may have decided that being warm and friendly were weaknesses and, therefore, while continuing to be aggressive, you no longer were as sympathetic or receptive.

Possibly you may, as a child, have been persistent and relentless. Then you went to school, were aggressive and some bigger child hit you or your teacher criticized you for speaking without permission. Embarrassed, you may have decided that you no longer were loved automatically for who you were, but only if you performed or achieved according to a structured pattern. Then you may have become, to some varying degree, inhibited.

Watch people who only speak when spoken to, who have lost the spontaneity of their inherent nature and the ability to be on stage, as the child they once were.

Decide what qualities you need to reacquire to return to the perfect child who is still within you. Do you need to become:

- More relentless in your persistence;
- More effective in your role playing;
- Quickly able to change techniques; or
- More disarming in your nature, so your persistence does not threaten people?

As an illustration, a child went to bed and, a moment later, called out, "Dad, can I have a glass of water?" His father replied, "You already had two glasses of water and one glass of juice, so get to sleep."

A moment later, the child asks, "Dad, can I have a glass of water?" His father said, "If you don't get to sleep, I am going to spank you."

A few moments later, "Can I have a glass of water?" More angrily, his father replied, "If you don't get to sleep, I will get a belt and spank you."

A moment later, "Dad, when you bring the belt, could you bring a glass of water?"

What can you do in such a situation? You may have no choice but to give the child what he or she requests, because the child is persevering in such a way that you have to be amused or at least disarmed.

Now give your own inner child the opportunity to be as expressive.

Be Spontaneous

For example, a real estate salesman at a workshop seminar that I was conducting in 1969 told the class that he was unable to prospect door-to-door for fear of being rejected. I explained to him that, because of being as sensitive as he was, all he needed to do was be spontaneous and, once people realized how personable and kind he was, they would automatically like him.

He said he would follow my suggestion. When he returned the following week, he described his experience. He had introduced himself to a lady as a real estate agent. She angrily responded, "All real estate people are crooks," and without thinking he held his suit jacket open and asked spontaneously, "Do you see a gun?" Then he explained how embarrassed he felt, yet she immediately began laughing.

Selling the Presidency

Possibly the most challenging product to sell is that of the presidency. Newspapers and television examine every characteristic of the candidate. The slightest error is magnified and critically studied.

In 1972, the American public was forced to choose between two very opposite personalities. George McGovern was warm and sensitive. He assured us that he cared about us. We felt we could trust him.

George McGovern, however, was not an aggressive or decisive person. He said he was 100 percent in favor of his initial choice for vice president, Tom Eagleton, but he frustrated his closest advisers with his inability to make a decision. On the whole, the American public felt he was someone who cared about them, but that he was not a strong personality who, in a crisis, could take care of them.

Then Richard Nixon convinced us, in his aggressive persistence and adamant determination, that he could take care of us. Yet many people did not feel he cared about us. We felt we could depend on him to deal aggressively with a crisis, but many believed we could not trust him. The term "Tricky Dicky" was not a 1974 Watergate term but appeared in the early 1950s.

When the American public was forced into a choice of extremes, they voted, by a landslide, for someone they could depend on rather then someone they could trust.

At a cocktail party or social gathering, you may prefer to be with someone you can relate to, such as George McGovern, rather than someone who would monologue, as Richard Nixon was accused of doing. When deciding between a presidential candidate you feel is a friend in whom you can trust or a father you can depend on, usually the father-type personality will get the vote.

Just as in the selling of the presidency, this concept applies in the selling of almost any product or service. The ideal situation is charisma, which is the balancing of the best qualities of both personalities in such a way that anyone can identify with you.

Think of Jack Kennedy who, despite his age, religion and the notoriety of his father, was able to come from behind and win in 1960. He was considered one of the most charismatic presidents, and his death emotionally overwhelmed a major percentage of the American public, let alone the entire world. He was a very aggressive person, determined and ambitious, yet his warmth and humor caused people to both trust and depend on him.

Ronald Reagan, as the president of the 1980s, captured that same balance. On television, he projected to the American public that he was a strong, confident person, yet with a smile and a sense of humor which caused people to feel very comfortable.

In the summer of 1988, George Bush was 17 points behind with a 40 percent negative rating. George was labeled a "wimp." The Doonesbury cartoon even had President Reagan being asked, "Does George have any strengths?", and he allegedly replied, "Yes, he never interrupts me." Suddenly, George became very aggressive, though Doonesbury claimed that it was not George who had made the personality change, but his evil twin brother Skippy.

George may have made a true personality change or possibly he was following the instructions of his campaign manager. Maybe he was returning to his old college days as a first baseman on the Yale baseball team when he played in the national championships two years in a row and was renewing his naturally aggressive, competitive spirit. All we know is that when George was in trouble, he had the ability to assure the majority of the American public that, under pressure, he could be decisive; and from 17 points behind, he won by eight percentage points.

Many years ago, a presidential candidate did not have to be charismatic to be elected. He would travel the country, speaking from the back of a train. The newspapers would print his speech and the voters usually would make their decisions according to the issues.

Today, elections are won and lost by the image the candidate projects in television debates and on the news programs. A primary factor in Jack Kennedy's election was Richard Nixon's physical appearance during the television debates and the use of, or lack of, cosmetics.

Ronald Reagan was referred to as the "Teflon President." If he made any statement that could cause criticism, it did not stick. His ability as an actor was ideal for television. The challenge of selling the presidency is the same challenge as selling any product. Today, we often communicate through television, such as video conferencing, or we need to make a presentation with charisma.

Think of how easy it is for you to react under pressure. When you were a child, and felt loved automatically for who you were, then being spontaneous and persistent may have been easy. In the future, if you can keep that balance, even when being rejected, you gradually will win people to your side.

DEVELOPING BALANCE

If you saw the movie *Working Girl*, you will remember that the heroine had high expectations. While she expected a great deal of herself, she was also a warm, sensitive person. In fact, she was so kind and pleasant that people were taking advantage of her. While they trusted her as a sincere and honest person, they would not give her any significant responsibility. Soon she was depressed and considering quitting.

Then she took on a position which did not belong to her and began acting as though she was an authority. People began to respect her. As they started depending on her, she began to succeed, and her success reinforced her new self-image and made her confidence real. This can be one of the most natural ways to develop your potential. You play the role and keep making corrections until you gain the desired response. Then you integrate the positive feedback into your self-image until you realize who you really are.

The best approach to accomplish your objective would be to merge the AIDA and Need-Satisfaction theories. You begin by gaining the attention and interest of the prospects, then discover their needs, gain their agreement regarding their requirements and finally create a desire for your product which culminates in satisfaction.

Yet attention and interest are part of establishing rapport, and you also have to focus on the presentation and overcoming objections. In addition, throughout the persuasion process, you need to think in terms of developing an ideal relationship and gaining results. If you are friendly, you will be effective in developing the relationship, and if you are aggressive, you will more likely succeed in gaining results. There are two ways to express your personality: either you are warm, friendly and relationship-oriented or aggressive, dominant and results-oriented. One way is emotional and enthusiastic and the other receptive and introspective.

You must determine which person is most effective within each of the stages of the sales process, as well as the style of each personality:

- When developing rapport, you want to be warm and friendly and express yourself with emotions and feeling.
- When determining the prospect's needs, you will want to continue to be sensitive and friendly. Yet this is a time when you need to listen and be receptive.
- If you need to alert the prospect to the seriousness of their situation, you want to speak with authority and confidence. To reduce the danger of threatening the person, however, your style needs to be calm and relaxed.
- When presenting solutions, you want to be personable and sincere, so the prospect feels your suggestions are for their benefit. You always want to be emotional and excited, for enthusiasm is contagious.
- When overcoming objections, the most effective person is strong and dominant, yet their impact on the prospect is softened by the salesperson's comfortable and calm style.
- When you decide the timing is right to close, you need to be confident and decisive, and in your effort to gain the prospect's agreement, you need to speak with feeling and emotions.

- Remembering the sale ends, not with the sale, but the customer's satisfaction, you need to follow up after the buying decision. You need to continue the rapport by being friendly and pleasant, in an emotional and expressive style.

The following chart lists the objectives of the selling process, when to be relationship-oriented and when to be results-oriented and whether you need to be emotional and expressive or calm and receptive:

The Seven Stages of the Selling Cycle	The Most Effective Personality	The Ideal Style
Establishing Rapport	Warm/Friendly	Emotions/Feeling
Determining Needs	Sensitive/Friendly	Listening/Receptive
Describing Reality	Authoritative/ Confident	Calm/Relaxed
Presenting Solutions	Personable/Sincere	Emotional/Excited
Overcoming Objections	Strong/Dominant	Comfortable/Calm
Closing	Confident/Decisive	Feelings/Emotions
Following Up	Friendly/Pleasant	Emotional/Expressive

6

Managing Resistance

Momentum is energy in continuous movement.

For many people in sales, the primary challenge is managing resistance. People would buy automatically if they desired our product and offered no objections. For example, a car manufacturer introduces a new model which becomes very desirable. People have to put their names on a waiting list. The car dealer may even raise the price thousands of dollars above the retail price and people still will gladly pay it.

CONFRONTING RESISTANCE

The challenge in selling is one of resistance. The prospect does not want to see us or speak to us. They do not agree with us when we claim that they need our product. If they do agree that they need to make a change, they may want to buy from our competitor. When we ask for a decision, they may object, and when we continue closing, they may become more resistant.

Once we understand the various objectives of the persuasion process that we need to achieve, and the reactions to failure, rejection and anxiety that are required to succeed in selling, then we are ready to develop those techniques which will disengage the prospect's resistance and gain their receptivity.

The prospect's first decision, if we are to make the sale is, "Do I want to see this salesperson?" From our sales-oriented perspective, therefore, the selling process begins with prospecting, whether door-to-door, by telephone or even by fax.

Prospecting, for a significant percentage of salespeople, is the most difficult challenge they confront. Their primary frustration is caused by the resistance they experience—in other words, rejection.

Many salespeople feel confident only when the prospect accepts them and becomes receptive. Then they move more easily through the various stages and onto frequent sales. Possibly, they feel that once they have established rapport, they can take a more aggressive position. Thus, the challenge is dealing with the initial resistance. How do we disengage the prospect's hostility and gain their receptivity?

GAINING AGREEMENT

The first law of prospecting is: *You have to try five times before you can expect to gain agreement.* If you place yourself in the prospect's position, you would readily agree that most people will not become responsive on your opening effort. On the average, you may have to try five times. Yet, how can you try five times without antagonizing the prospective client? The prospect, for example, may react with frustration, "I've said no three times. Now, will you leave me alone?" Of course, you could respond by saying, "But, I only have two to go." This, however, is not suggested. The solution is referred to as *downward incremental pressure.* In other words, on each attempt to gain agreement, ask for less, until by the fifth effort, if not sooner, the prospect cannot help but agree with you because your request is so reasonable.

Think of five ways that you can gain agreement. You now will be given many different ways to gain agreement.

First, however, consider two factors that determine which techniques are most appropriate.

The Prospect's Receptivity

The first factor is the prospect. Every prospect will react within a spectrum of resistance, in which one side is receptivity and the other side is hostility.

Also realize that all selling techniques, whether they are for prospecting, overcoming objections, closing or any aspect of the selling process, will be either aggressive or gentle or varying degrees of both.

If a prospect is receptive to you, then you can afford to become more aggressive. For example, if the prospect says, "I believe you have a great product," you can feel comfortable in saying, "If you like it, then do you want to acquire the super deluxe model?"

In contrast, if the prospect is particularly hostile and says, "You are the tenth person to call today, now leave me alone," then you will have to use gentle techniques to disengage this hostility. In other words, you are in no position to be selling your product if the prospect is being resistant. If the prospect is hostile, then your first objective is to develop rapport and gain their receptivity.

Your Resiliency

The second primary factor when determining which of the aggressive or gentle techniques are most appropriate is your ego. During every moment of the day, your ego is somewhere within a spectrum of resiliency and vulnerability.

If you are having a bad day and are feeling vulnerable, then you will want to use gentle techniques. In this way, you can continue trying, but with an approach which is less likely to irritate the prospect and cause them to reject you. In other words, the more sensitive you feel, the more you want to increase the rapport and reduce the prospect's resistance before becoming aggressive. If you are resilient and rejection may only amuse you, however, then you can afford to use aggressive techniques.

From another perspective, decide what objective you want to achieve—developing the relationship or gaining results. If you have yet to create the appropriate relationship, then you need to use gentle techniques. If the timing is appropriate for seeking results, then you will want to use more aggressive techniques.

Trying for the Sale

The first technique for gaining agreement is the actual sale. Take your favorite product, possibly one which is easy to sell or you particularly believe in, and just go for it.

The odds of the prospect buying with this direct-selling effort, of course, are minimal. Consider the purpose of using a technique which invariably generates a negative reaction.

Each of us comes in contact with about 1,800 sales messages per day. If that figure seems high, then think of how many advertisements you will see whenever you read a newspaper page. You scan the pages and avoid looking at the advertisements while reading the titles of the articles, deciding which are of interest. You have to see the advertisement for a fraction of a second, however, to decide that you will not read it. Hundreds of times a day you are saying, while reading newspapers and magazines, let alone observing other media such as billboards, television and radio commercials, as well as other sales messages, "No, I do not want to look at or listen to you."

Remember Pavlov's dog. When the dog was fed, a bell would ring. After awhile, just ringing the bell would cause the dog to salivate. People are the same. Whenever they suspect that someone is trying to sell them they automatically will say no. Their spontaneous resistance is a conditioned reflex.

CREATING RECEPTIVITY

Your first objective in selling, therefore, is not to sell the product, nor to sell yourself or even to try to set up an appointment. Your first objective is to *eliminate the prospect's fear of being threatened, to disengage their protective devices, so the prospect will be receptive to your suggestions.*

Think of the various ways in which you can accomplish this objective. One way would be to first allow the prospect to say no. In other words, let the prospect express resistance. If you use clever techniques that force a positive response, the prospect often will feel that they are being "set up" or manipulated, and this will only solidify their resistance.

When you begin the conversation by telling the prospect about a great idea you have for them, and even discuss benefits, but the prospect still says no, listen to their degree of resistance. If the prospect is really hostile, you know that your next technique must be gentle. If the prospect's reaction is negative yet somewhat receptive, such as, "That sounds interesting, but I am busy at this time," then you can use a more aggressive technique, such as asking to visit with the prospect when they are more relaxed.

A primary strength in selling is to disengage your ego from rejection while remaining sensitive to the prospect's reaction. Only then can you use good judgment to decide what technique to use next. Too often, salespeople are sensitive regarding their own egos and consider the prospect's negative reactions as rejection. Successful people have strong egos which allow them to be sensitive to the prospect's feelings, understand the reason for the negative feedback and change their strategy to gain the prospect's acceptance.

More specifically, one of your primary objectives when prospecting is to *seek agreement on every call.* Of course, you will not always gain agreement, but at least make the effort.

When striving to gain agreement on every call, the agreement does not have to be the actual buying decision, as desirable as that might be. But you do want to at least create a reason to call back. Most prospects will not buy from you until they feel comfortable with you.

You want them to feel that you both care about them and can take care of them. Obviously, a quick conversation on the telephone usually is not enough to assure a prospect that he or she can trust you and also depend on you, particularly when selling complex products. Your initial contact, therefore, is only the first step in establishing the kind of relationship which will culminate in the desired results.

The Appointment

Do not be surprised if, in your opening effort to sell your product, the prospect says, "I can't believe your timing. I'm ready to buy." If you make enough calls then, merely by the percentages, you may experience some success. If the person does not buy, however, then your second technique to gain agreement is to ask for an appointment, such as, "Could I have lunch with you, or perhaps breakfast? I would like to make your acquaintance." or "How about avoiding rush-hour traffic some afternoon and let me review some ideas with you?"

Promotional Material

If the prospect says yes, you have achieved your objective. You have gained agreement and are developing a relationship. If the prospect says, "I don't want to see you," then move on to your third technique: "Could I at least mail you some information on this new idea and call you back for your opinion?"

Do not mail literature unless the prospect agrees that you can call for their evaluation. If the person agrees, then ask when you can call again to get their feedback.

Meeting an Assistant

If the person is negative and says, "I don't want to see you, and I don't want to read your literature," then try the fourth technique, which is attempting to speak to someone in a staff or advisory position by saying:

> I can understand why you don't want to deal with me, for you are a very successful person, and people as important as you are usually have someone who takes care of these matters for them. Could I speak to your assistant [your financial adviser, your spouse, your purchasing agent, etc.]. If I find that you do not need me, I will send you a letter telling you so, and if I discover a way to help you, the letter will only be one page, outlining what I can do for you. Would that be reasonable, to be able to speak to your support person?

Often, salespeople prefer that the decision maker not be available when they call, for then they have the opportunity to speak to someone who is in a staff position. An assistant generally offers little sales resistance, for salespeople rarely contact them. They often are receptive and may give you valuable information, such as the nature of the decision maker, their needs, the present supplier, the budget and future objectives.

It is only reasonable that you want to understand the prospect's needs and frustrations before contacting them. The less complex your product, the less research is required. If you are selling sophisticated products, however, then you want to speak with someone in a staff position to do the necessary research. You need to be as knowledgeable as possible regarding all the factors which eventually will determine the buying decision. Only then are you ready to meet the prospective client.

Often the decision maker is concerned with more serious responsibilities and thus delegates the product analysis to someone in a support position. The decision maker also may base their decision on the recommendations of their administrative assistant. For example, consider the percentage of wealthy doctors who take the time to analyze their financial and insurance needs and evaluate the various available products and services. Invariably, their spouses, tax advisers or accountants gather the information before they make a decision. They may even ask this person to make the decision for them.

Just because the prospect does not want to see or speak with you is not a reason to avoid your objective. A prospect's negative feedback is your opportunity to try a different technique. Meet with someone in a staff position, gather information and prepare yourself to meet with the decision maker.

OTHER PROSPECTING APPROACHES

Before moving on to the next technique, you need to acknowledge the variety of prospecting strategies which complement or conflict with this approach.

For example, certain salespeople claim that you must first qualify the prospect, determine that he or she has the money to invest, then ask if the prospect will consider buying your recommendations. Otherwise, try another prospect.

Similarly, some sales trainers insist that you should never mention a product until you have determined the prospect's needs, while others believe that an opening statement that outlines a benefit of your product to gain their attention and interest is the appropriate way to initiate the conversation.

Often salespeople are told that if the prospect is negative, then they should end the conversation, thus rejecting the prospect. In other words, why allow a person to continue being hostile to you when there are "so many fish in the sea"?

Of course, many factors determine the ideal prospecting strategy. One primary factor, as previously discussed, is the product. If you are selling a product as simple as magazine subscriptions, then almost everyone is a prospect, and you can move quickly through your prospecting list, seeking only receptive people.

If you are marketing sophisticated products, such as computer technology or financial services, however, then your list of qualified prospects usually will be limited. You do not want a competitor succeeding, merely because you could not deal with the prospect's negative feedback.

Consider the quarterback who goes into the first huddle and says, "I am confident we are going to succeed. When I go back to pass, I want ten targets downfield." This quarterback will be a hero or badly damaged. He is wide open, with no protection. In selling, you need a strong defense to deal with hostile prospects; yet you do not want to be so protective that you become unproductive. In other words, do not get your defense in the way of your offense.

Back to the quarterback who, trying for the long pass without protection, soon is battered and bruised. In the huddle he says, "I've had it. I cannot stand anymore pain. When I go back to pass, I want all ten of you back with me. We are going to create the wagon-train defense. All of you entwine arms and encircle me, and then we will shuffle downfield; but we are not going anywhere until I know I am protected."

This quarterback may not be hurt again, but he may not get very far. Whether you are playing chess or football or are selling, you need a good offense to produce and a strong defense to protect. And you need both at the same time. Think of the type of defense that protects you from hostility balanced by an offense which allows you to extend yourself to be productive.

Within the proposed prospecting strategy is both your ego protection and your sales production. As you seek a point of agreement, you need to read the defense (monitor the prospect's reactions) and then make high-speed changes (modify your technique). By being sensitive to the prospect's reactions, you can decide what your next request will be. You will understand what request will be reasonable, as you try to gain some form of agreement. Thus, with a reason to call back, the relationship will begin to develop, and the opportunity for the desired results increases.

Think of the quarterback who, having decided on his game plan, finds his target downfield has stumbled and four men weighing a total of 1,200 pounds are moving toward him at high speed. What does he do?

Does he walk off the field, tell his coach that the other side is being disrespectful and throw down the ball? Of course not. Instead, he enjoys the challenge of making a quick change in his strategy, such as passing off or scrambling. As much as he would like to score a touchdown on every play, he accepts the reality of his challenge: to make a first down by the third play. You also need to gain agreement—a reason to call again—by the fifth try in your effort to score.

If you are selling sophisticated services and complex products, you must be able to study the various strategies which are available in prospecting. Then experiment and develop an approach which is ideal for your personality, the product you are selling and the prospect you have contacted.

Conducting Seminars

Returning to the proposed prospecting strategy of *downward incremental pressure,* we move on to the fifth technique for gaining agreement, which is seminars. The best way to sell often is to stop selling and conduct seminars.

When you are selling, people will perceive you as a salesperson. When you conduct seminars, people will view you as a consultant, adviser or authority, which you really are or want to be. If you feel uncomfortable presenting seminars, either for lack of product knowledge or for fear of speaking in front of a group, then find competent, charismatic people who will make the presentation. Then you can introduce the speaker and end the program with a few words which can result in appointments and new accounts.

You can contact a local college and present your seminars as part of the evening adult-education program. You can contact service clubs, such as a Rotary club, a women's professional group or a chamber of commerce. These groups benefit from charging a nominal fee and increase the exposure of their organizations to increasing their memberships. Some of your associates can work with you on a team basis.

With a seminar schedule, you can deal more easily with hostile prospects. If the prospect is negative toward you, then you can say:

> By the way, I am presenting a seminar this Wednesday in co-sponsorship with the Junior College. An expert is speaking on this new approach that I believe might be worthwhile for you. Would you like to be my guest?

Immediately, you have upgraded your image in the marketplace. This technique also gives you an opportunity to reduce the prospect's resistance, develop an effective relationship and increase your chances of eventual results.

Reference Selling

The sixth technique for gaining agreement is reference selling. For example:

> I met with your neighbor, Jim Jackson, and his wife last Wednesday night, and they were so pleased with how I was able to help them that they suggested I call the people next door. If you don't trust me, then ask Jim about me and I'll call again in a couple of weeks. If you do feel comfortable with me, then could I meet with you next Wednesday night?

In this last approach, you are using two techniques to gain agreement. One is asking for the appointment, which is the more aggressive technique. If the prospect is receptive, then such an approach would be appropriate. If the prospect is resistant or hostile, then the more gentle approach, which is the reference-selling technique, generally will gain the prospect's trust and agreement.

Referral Selling

The seventh technique, which is an even less-threatening approach, is referral selling. In this technique, you try to disengage the prospect's resistance by no longer selling. In other words, if the prospect is unreceptive, then respond to this resistance by asking, "Since you obviously do not need me, then maybe there is someone you know who could benefit from what I have to offer?" This is as though you are saying, "I give up. I am no longer selling, so you can relax. Rather than seeing me as a stranger, I hope you will now see me as a friend who needs your help."

Remember, when you are selling, people start protecting themselves. When you stop selling, they no longer will feel a need to be resistant and often will become receptive.

Words and their meanings often are different subjects. When you say, "Since you do not need me, maybe you know someone who could benefit from my service," the prospect most likely will think, "I'm off the hook. I don't have to keep protecting myself."

Therefore, what you really said is, "You are too tough for me. I am no longer trying to sell to you."

Free Services

The eighth technique is providing free services. What can you offer a prospect which might eliminate resistance and help you establish rapport? You might distribute a newsletter, or you might conduct a free analysis of a prospect's situation. You could do research for them, regarding information they need.

Obviously, this gentle technique is for those prospects who are so negative that all other techniques are failing. This approach is appropriate when the potential business is significant and the selling cycle is lengthy.

Time

The ninth technique is time: "Since you don't need me now, is there a time in the future that I may call you, just to see if your situation has changed?"

Imagine that in your opening effort the prospect says, "I'm really angry. Where is my secretary that I have to answer my own telephone? I'm sorry, but I'm in a meeting and I can't speak to you."

Think of the prospect's reaction. Is it hostile? Actually not, for while the prospect is angry, the hostility is not directed toward you but toward their secretary. What the prospect actually said was "I'm sorry,...but I can't speak to you."

Thus, you can be somewhat aggressive in your response by asking, "Well then, could I call you this afternoon or tomorrow?"

If the prospect said angrily, "What list am I on that you people are irritating me all day long?", then you need to be very gentle and reply, "I'm sorry for having irritated you, but is there a time when I may call you when you are not so upset, such as six months from now or possibly next year?"

Seek agreement by determining which request will be acceptable to the prospect. Reduce the pressure so that your request becomes so reasonable that the prospect cannot continue to resist. Disarm the prospect's hostility and increase their receptivity. Monitor the prospect's feeling and modify your approach.

Persevere and be patient. If you persevere without patience, you probably will be successful but frustrated. If you are patient without perseverance, you usually will be relaxed, but you may not succeed. You need both qualities at the same time. Balance is the answer.

Specifically, each year, from the first of January to the early days of November, if anyone is angry or hostile toward you, and all your efforts are futile, then ask, "Could I at least call you at Christmastime to see how you are doing?" or "Could I call you during the holidays in December and see what your plans are for next year?"

People have great difficulty being Scrooges during Christmas. You usually will gain a positive response to this gentle request.

Also, the December holiday season usually is the worst time of the year to sell but the best time of the year to establish rapport, develop good relationships and gain agreement with a prospect regarding when you can meet with him or her.

If the prospect is hostile toward your request of future contact, however, and says, "Never call me again," then you may ask humorously, "Could I call you five years from now?"

This tenth technique is one of humor. In other words, try to break the tension by being absurd. If all else fails, this last technique just may work.

In review, open with an idea you are excited about to gain a reaction. Then use techniques two through eight, choosing those three which seem most appropriate in gaining agreement. The ninth technique, time, is used on the fifth effort. The tenth technique, using humor, is optional, and would be used on a sixth effort.

Be flexible. Feel comfortable using any of the techniques for an opener, such as reference selling, "Your friend, Tom, was so pleased with how I helped him, that he suggested I call you." You could combine techniques on your opening approach, such as setting up the appointment and providing literature: "I would like to meet with you and review some ideas or, if you are too busy, I could send you some information for your evaluation. Would that be reasonable? Which would you prefer?"

When selling, you often do not know how receptive or resistant a prospect might be. One way to measure a prospect's feeling toward you is to make a request and then ask two more questions and observe which one he or she answers: "Does this seem reasonable?" or "Have I said anything that is distracting you?"

If the prospect agrees to any one of your earlier requests, then ask a question of time. For example, if the prospect agrees to read your literature, then thank him or her and finish by asking, "...and when should I call back for your opinion?"

If the prospect agrees that you can contact their assistant or spouse, then express your appreciation and ask, "...and when should I call you again to review what I discussed with your assistant?"

Be relentless, but also be sensitive to the prospect's reaction. Monitor any resistance and modify your approach so that your request is so reasonable that the prospect becomes receptive.

More important than the actual prospecting technique is that you make the call. Activity that is productive, rather than protective, usually will create results. Too often, salespeople make calls for the sake of activity rather than results.

You want to evaluate your personality and develop a prospecting approach which keeps you on the telephone or in the field with your prospects to gain results rather than just to appear active.

Certain salespeople develop very effective prospecting techniques that often elicit positive responses from people who are not really interested. Then these salespeople may spend a great deal of their time on appointments with people whom they "charmed" into an appointment, but who are not really interested. These people, after having been persuaded into setting up appointments, often may become resentful and even belligerent.

Correspondingly, some salespeople purposely may use a technique that is so nonpersuasive that the only people who ever would set up appointments already are very receptive. For example, "My name is Art Mortell, and I sell life insurance. If you have all the life insurance you need, then just tell me. I don't want to irritate you."

This technique, on a percentage basis, will elicit few positive responses, but those who react positively usually will be aware of their needs and receptive when the agent arrives.

Decide, based on the complexity of your product and the number of qualified prospects in your area, how persuasive your prospecting approach needs to be. If you are selling a noncomplex product and you have a relatively unlimited number of prospects, then you may want to use techniques that will help you quickly sort out those people who are receptive to you and your product. Correspondingly, if you are marketing complex products and you have few qualified prospects, you may need to be well prepared when making the initial contact. You may want to use a technique which reduces resistance, increases receptivity and assures you of at least gaining the prospect's agreement for you to call again.

For example, if you are selling financial services and you only want to sell stocks to those who enjoy some form of risk when investing, and your immediate objective is to open new accounts, then you use a technique which helps you contact prospects quickly. If, instead, your objective is to develop strong relationships with qualified prospects who offer the opportunity of earning significant incomes, then you may want to find a point of agreement which allows you to meet with the person, gain their confidence and trust, and evolve into a permanent relationship with significant results.

As an illustration of the need to match the prospecting techniques with the dynamics of the marketing environment, imagine someone selling supercomputers, with only one qualified prospect, such as a major automobile manufacturer or a state government. The salesperson makes the initial contact, using an aggressive technique, confronts immediate rejection and returns to the office, explaining to the sales manager, "I didn't hit it off with the contact. I need another prospect."

The challenge is to monitor the prospect's reactions to understand the nature of any resistance. Then modify your approach to gain some form of receptivity. The agreement might be as simple as meeting with someone in a staff position who will provide you with the information which allows you to develop a viable strategy.

Self-Competition

One technique which can keep you consistent in your prospecting is *self-competition*. With this motivational technique, you reduce the stress of selling by temporarily disregarding results. Rather than being concerned about new accounts, making quota and your financial objectives, you focus only on activity.

Activity and Results

If the following assumption applies to you, then the technique probably will help you: If your activity is consistent, the results usually will follow.

More specifically, whenever you make a prospecting call, if the prospect is not available, you score one point. If the prospect speaks with you but is negative, you score two points. If you gain some form of agreement, such as the prospect agreeing to an appointment or evaluating your literature, then you score three points. Your objective is to score as many points as possible in a day.

Creating Momentum

One of the most powerful forces in our lives is momentum, which I define as "energy in continuous movement." When your energy is negative, you may wonder to yourself, "Will I ever do well?" When your energy is positive, you may feel like King Midas, with the golden touch.

The way to create momentum in your life is not to worry about how many points you score in a day, as long as you score one more point than you did yesterday.

Competing with Yourself

Too often, if you compete with someone who is more successful, you only become more aware of your own shortcomings. Equally, if you compete with people who are not doing as well as you are, then you may feel no sense of challenge and lose some of your determination.

Instead, you need to compete with yourself. More specifically, you need to compete with the person you were yesterday.

For example, yesterday you may have scored 76 points. It is now four o'clock in the afternoon and you are emotionally exhausted. You check your score, determining that 20 people were unavailable (20 points), 15 people were negative (30 points) and eight people agreed to one of your requests (24 points) for a total of 74 points.

You need two more points for a tie, and one more for momentum. You make two more calls, and no one is available. You need just one more point. You make the call, the person is available and you say, "My name is Mark Johnson. I'm a stockbroker, and you probably do not need me, do you?" (all you want to do is go home) and he says, "I can't believe your timing. How about meeting with me and my accountant tomorrow regarding my corporation retirement plan?" You say, "but I need only one more point."

Selling is a game in which you compete with yourself. Rejection no longer exists, and your vulnerabilities are disengaged. Rejection becomes a statistical experience, in which the more you are rejected, the more you succeed. Rejection, therefore, is only a numbers game—one of self-competition.

7

Overcoming Objections

*Eliminate the prospect's fear of being threatened to
disengage their protective devices, so the prospect
will be receptive to your suggestions.*

When selling, you confront a continuous challenge of resistance, beginning with an initial prospecting effort, through the closing process and even into the concern of buyer's remorse. Yet the primary focus in overcoming objections occurs between giving the presentation and seeking the buying decision. If the prospect accepts your proposal, the buying decision may follow automatically. Your responsibility is to anticipate any objections and to present your products in such a way that you resolve the prospect's concerns in advance. You also want to provide solutions that create enthusiasm and allow the close to occur easily. When you present solutions, first list the primary features of your product. Remember, however, that people do not buy the features of a product but the advantages and the benefits which the product offers. Thus, you need to translate the features of your product into advantages and benefits and then ask for a response. If the prospect responds positively, you are ready to try your first closing technique. If the prospect responds negatively, continue to deal with any objections and present solutions until the prospect becomes receptive.

When presenting solutions, use the FABR technique, which is:

- Feature,
- Advantage,
- Benefit, and
- Response.

For example, "My car *features* a cruise control. The *advantage* is that you can drive without placing your foot on the gas pedal. The *benefits* are many. You drive more relaxed, maintain a steady speed and, therefore, reduce the danger of getting a speeding ticket. Now, how do you feel about these benefits?"

UNDERSTANDING THE OBJECTION

If the prospect says, "Scares the heck out of me," obviously the prospect has an objection. The first step to resolve an objection is to determine its true nature.

A significant percentage of objections are not real, but only are defenses which prospective clients use to protect themselves. Often, the prospect may not even know why he or she feels negative and does not want to buy.

Therefore, to overcome objections, you first want to determine the prospect's real feelings. Do not assume that the objection is what really is upsetting the prospect. The way to determine the prospect's true feelings is to use a technique referred to as *rephrase in question form*. Specifically, take the prospect's objection and repeat their words in question form. Do not add or change words. If you make any change, then reduce the words to make the technique more subtle and, thus, more effective

For example, if the prospect objects by saying, "It's just too expensive," do not ask, "Why do you feel it is too expensive?" This only forces the prospect to justify their position.

THE NEED TO DEFEND

More specifically, understand that the prospect has two needs whenever he or she voices an objection. The first need is one you want to avoid, which is the prospect's need to protect himself or herself. When you ask, "Tell me why you feel it is too expensive?", you are forcing the prospect to justify any negative feelings. If the objection is not the prospect's real concern, then you are forcing the prospect to crystallize objections which do not exist.

THE NEED TO EXPRESS FEELINGS

What you want to touch is the prospect's need to express any negative feelings. Take a prospect's objection, such as, "It's too expensive," and merely rephrase the objection in question form. Just ask, "Too expensive?", and keep your voice gentle and inquisitive, rather than challenging or demanding. In other words, you really are saying, "I'm confused and want to understand why you feel this way."

The prospect may respond by saying, "I am embarrassed to tell you, but my mother-in-law actually is paying for this, and I've got to get her permission" or "The CEO makes these decisions, and I should have told you up front that while it should be my responsibility, he is the one to decide."

By understanding what really is upsetting the prospect, the appropriate response on your part may become obvious.

Of course, the initial objection might be the real objection. For example, the prospect may say, "Yes, it is too expensive. Look at this proposal from your competition. Their prices are much lower."

If you had asked, "Could you show me my competitor's proposal, so I may see what their prices are?", the prospect may tell you, "Of course not." If you ask, "Too expensive?", however, the prospect may respond to your gentle inquisitiveness and show you what you are up against.

As one more illustration, the prospect may object by saying, "I'm sorry, but it's just not the right time." You reply, "Not the right time?", and the prospect says, "That's right. We just finished our last purchase and the next budget will not be finalized for another six months."

You realize that this is the true objection. Now you can more easily develop ways to resolve the resistance you are confronting, such as, "When would be an appropriate time to call you back, when you will have an idea of what you plan on doing?" If the prospect suggests that you contact them in four months, then ask, "Could I send you material on this product? I would appreciate your evaluation."

If the prospect accepts your literature, then call two weeks later, saying, "I just wanted to make sure you received the promotional material."

If the prospect acknowledges receiving it, then ask, "Could I meet with you to review your opinion of my program, possibly for lunch if you would prefer?"

Gradually, you are converting any objections into your opportunity to develop a relationship with the prospect which will increase your chances to gain eventual results.

Feel, Felt and Found

The classic technique for overcoming objections is Feel, Felt, Found and Response. More specifically, when someone objects, do not respond by saying, "Yes, but...", for you will not seem sincere if your "but" is expressed immediately.

Rather, you need to condition yourself to say, "Yes, I know how you *feel*. I once, in fact, *felt* the same way. I had a customer who had the same problem which you are afraid will occur. Therefore, because of my experience with such situations, I have *found*, if you do it this way instead, the problem is resolved before it occurs." Then you always ask for a response, such as, "Does that make sense to you?" or "Does that resolve your concern?"

If the prospect responds negatively, then explore the objections more thoroughly. If the prospect voices another objection, then follow this same procedure: Ask for an explanation and again use Feel, Felt and Found. For example, you are selling the benefits of a cruise control and the prospect says, "Scares the heck out of me." You inquisitively would respond, "Scares the heck out of you?" and if the prospect says, "Yes, you have no control of the car. It's driving automatically," then you would know their objection is real. You then would say, "I understand your concern. I have talked to many people with the same apprehensions. However, you can control the car whenever you wish, by stepping on the gas to accelerate or on the brakes to stop. In fact, with this cruise control, while the car is driving for you, you can keep your foot by the brakes and react even more quickly in an emergency. Now, does that resolve your concerns?"

If the prospect responds positively—"Yes, that does resolve my concerns"—then move on to your next FABR or try a closing technique.

In fact, the only real problem when using the Feel, Felt and Found technique is that you may do better than you expected.

> For example, a man received a call from his wife that his son's turtle had died and that he should come home early and console his son.
>
> When the father arrived home, he was prepared. He said to his son, "I know just how you *feel*. I once *felt* the same, when my pet canary died. However, because of this experience, I have *found* that if we find a pretty place in the backyard for your turtle, ask your friends over for some hymns and prayers and then serve cake and ice cream, you will feel better."
>
> His son seemed happier, as they built a little coffin and dug a tiny grave. Then Dad said, "Johnny, in preparation for your friends' arrival, get the turtle," so Johnny brought the turtle to his father. When he handed the turtle to his father, the turtle moved, and Dad said, "Look, Johnny, your turtle is still alive."
>
> And Johnny said, "Dad, let's kill it."

Now that is not a pleasant story, but it does illustrate that the technique of Feel, Felt and Found works so well that you may do better than you expected.

In another example, consider the martial arts of jujitsu. If you are attacked by someone, you do not counterattack, stand there and take it nor run away. Instead, you follow a four-step process:

1. *React with concern* by asking questions such as, "What have I said to upset you, so I will not make the same error in the future?" or "Have you had a bad experience with someone like me?" As the person expresses any negative feelings, their hostility may gradually
2. *Dissipate,* until they become
3. *Disarmed* and therefore
4. *Receptive* to your suggestions.

Many salespeople believe that objections should be disregarded. Supposedly, if you continue to present the benefits of your product and create enthusiasm, the prospect will forget any apprehensions and buy. While this approach may succeed when selling simple products, the appropriate approach is to anticipate the objections and prepare accordingly.

As you gain experience in your business, you will become familiar with the types of objections that prospects experience. If you understand the prospect's fears, you can develop a presentation which resolves the prospect's concerns before they are expressed.

While the presentation might be that moment in the selling process when objections are most likely to occur, sales resistance can occur within any stage of the sales cycle. For example, if you consistently confront the same objection in your prospecting calls, such as, "I'm satisfied with my present system," then begin your prospecting call by saying, "You probably are satisfied with your present system. However, I would appreciate if you would evaluate my program."

CRITERIA SELLING

If the prospect at any time throughout the conversation tells you that he or she is not ready to make a decision because the person has yet to evaluate a competitive product, then understand the important selling technique referred to as Criteria Selling.

Imagine a shoe salesman who has just been told by a prospect that, before she makes a decision, she wants to visit another shoe store and evaluate what it has to offer. The salesman, knowing the features, advantages and benefits of his brand, and the differences that exist between his shoes and those of his competitor's, now sets the criteria:

> I have enjoyed meeting you, and if by chance I never see you again, let me mention that whenever you are buying shoes, you must look for three items. First, notice the stitching on the shoes, which is very important if you want them to last. Shoes must have this type of stitching. Second, feel the leather cushioning. Without it you soon will feel as if you are walking barefoot on cement. Third, notice the construction of the heels and how it minimizes the chance of breaking. From this day on, whenever you buy shoes, make sure they have these three benefits.

Then when the lady visits another store and tries on shoes that do not have these three features, it is as though the salesperson is still with her, because he set the criteria which still is in her mind.

You need two primary qualities to succeed in selling. The first is to *monitor* the prospect's feelings, which requires that rather than being sensitive to yourself, you are sensitive to the prospect's reactions. If the reaction is negative, the salesperson must understand the nature of the prospect's resistance to decide what technique to use next.

CAPITALIZING ON NEGATIVE FEEDBACK

The second primary quality in selling is to *modify* your techniques, so you reduce the prospect's resistance until he or she eventually is receptive to you.

As an illustration, consider the modern torpedo. First it decides what target it wants to reach. Second, it sends out signals. Then its sensing device receives feedback which tells the torpedo if it is off course or on target. Finally, if the feedback is negative, the torpedo will make course corrections to get back on target.

Now imagine a torpedo which has an ego, and every time it receives negative feedback it takes it personally. What will the torpedo do?

It may go around in circles, waiting for something positive to happen. Salespeople often function in the same way. If they become oversensitive, they may take the negative feedback too personally and begin to go around in circles. In other words, they protect themselves from any further negative feedback, which they are assuming to be rejection, by procrastinating. Are you ever caught in that protective process?

Another negative option for the torpedo is to go to the bottom, as salespeople frequently do when they feel overwhelmed. They actually quit or at least disappear for a while. They sleep late, go to a movie in the afternoon or appear to be making prospecting calls when they actually are discussing with their friends a social gathering for the weekend.

The torpedo may go back home, which would be disastrous to the submarine. Yet that is often what salespeople do. They go back home and ask their spouses to support them, at least temporarily.

The torpedo may become overheated by taking the negative feedback too personally and blow up. Salespeople often will do the same. If they blow up externally, they become angry, such as yelling at a secretary or becoming abusive with their families when they get home. If they blow up internally, then this may result in suicide or overdosing on drugs or abusing alcohol. This often happens to people who cannot deal effectively with the stress.

Another negative option for the torpedo is to continue on its original course, oblivious to the feedback, miss the target and hit another only by accident. Salespeople often react with the same pattern. They employ one prospecting technique. They disregard any negative feedback and just keep on moving. If the prospect hangs up, they make their next call. If they have enough targets then, by merely playing the percentages, they will hit one.

Successful salespeople, just as the modern torpedo, enjoy the negative feedback. Their egos, which are their sensing devices, are sensitive, but not oversensitive. They are able to *monitor* the negative feedback and *modify* their techniques to keep moving in the right direction until they reach their objectives. In other words, they appreciate the negative feedback as the information they need to reach their targets.

8

The Challenge of Closing

*The buying decision is the result of providing the necessary
information and resolving objections.*

Probably the most important part of the selling process is closing. Two primary problems occur within this stage of selling. The
most frequent difficulty is asking for a decision. In other words, for
fear of rejection we do not close.

The second problem is the fear of failure, which causes certain
salespeople to close too often, too hard or too late. In other words,
the fear of losing control or not getting the order negatively affects
our timing.

If you are not sure which of these two problems is affecting you,
then consider the following test. If one of two experiences were to occur to you, which would you prefer:

- To fail at something important, but have people tell you how
  much they still love you and how courageous you were to
  have tried, or
- To achieve something significant and have people resent you
  and tell you, "I knew you would succeed, considering how
  ruthless and insensitive you are."

If these were your only choices, which one would you prefer?
Many people would decide: "I'd rather achieve and have people resent me."

Most people, if they are honest, however, will admit: "I'd rather fail and have people still like me."

If you would rather fail and be loved, you are probably a sensitive person who is so people-oriented that you may often sacrifice your own goals in life just to protect a relationship. Correspondingly, if you would rather achieve and be resented, you are most likely an aggressive person who is so goal-oriented that you may often sacrifice relationships just to assure your success.

How may your answer to these conflicting questions determine your behavior in such challenging responsibilities as business, selling and, even more specifically, closing?

AVOIDING THE CLOSE

If you are a sensitive person, who would rather fail and be loved, then you may not close for fear of rejection. Have you ever, when it was time to close, heard a voice in your mind saying, Don't close, for if you try the prospect may say, "I know a closing technique when I see one. I thought you were a nice person and that you cared about me; but you obviously are a salesperson. The only reason why you discussed the picture of my family was to manipulate me and take my money from me."

The sensitive salesperson, never wanting people to believe that their friendliness was only a manipulative device, may never close. Instead, they will continue in friendly conversation and hope the prospect will buy spontaneously, rather than attempt to close and perhaps be rejected.

BEING TOO AGGRESSIVE

The aggressive, dominant salesperson would rather achieve and be resented. Such power-oriented people believe that "a sale begins with a close, it ends with a close and we have to be closing everywhere in between, because when people have money, that money belongs to us. And when the prospect buys from us, then lean forward and say, 'I want three referrals from you. I'm not leaving here until I get them, and I need the names of people who are more successful than you are.' "

These people often do very well in selling. Frequently, however, they antagonize people, which causes cancellations, buyer's remorse and no repeat business.

Are you a warm, friendly person who, for fear of rejection, may have difficulty closing, or are you a strong, dominant person who, for fear of failing, closes too aggressively and too frequently, and therefore threatens people?

Regardless of whether you have difficulty closing, for fear of rejection, or you are closing too aggressively, for fear of losing, the closing techniques that now will be presented can resolve both problems. First, you cannot be rejected when using these five closing techniques. Second, the prospects will tell you what they are thinking, so your timing always will be accurate, rather than closing too often, too hard or too late.

If you understand how these techniques were developed, then you are more likely to use them more effectively. Many years ago, the advertising industry conducted research to determine how many times a selling message had to be presented to the same prospective customer before he or she would buy the product. The number was five.

The advertising industry then determined what the people were thinking whenever they read or listened to a sales message. The objective of the advertising industry was to better understand the type of messages it required to deal with the resistance it was confronting with each selling effort. Again, if we understand the person's resistance, we can develop techniques which will disengage any negative feelings and increase the prospect's receptivity to our ideas.

CREATING AWARENESS

The advertising industry discovered that on the first selling effort, the prospect will think, 'I was not aware that it was time to make a decision. We were having a pleasant conversation. This salesperson presented an idea, which I expressed some interest in. Then he asked me for a decision. I now am aware that it is time to decide what I want to do.'

The first word, therefore, which is the core of your first closing technique, is *awareness.*

DEVELOPING INTEREST

If the person says no to your first close, try a second time. The prospect then thinks, 'OK. I am aware that it's time to decide what I want to do, but am I interested in making a decision at this time?'

Thus the second word is *interest*. In this discussion, the word "interest" deals not with whether or not the prospect is interested in buying, but merely if he or she is interested in making a decision.

EVALUATING THE PRODUCT

If the prospective client says no, you try a third time, at which time the prospect may think, 'OK, I am interested in making a decision, but have I properly evaluated this product?' Your third word, therefore, is *evaluate*.

ANALYZING THE PROPOSAL

On your fourth try, the prospect may think, 'I've evaluated this person's recommendation, but this is not a casual decision. Have I thoroughly analyzed the proposal?' Then he or she says no, to keep you at arm's length, so you try a fifth time. The fourth word, however, is *analyze*.

ADOPTING THE SERVICE

On your fifth effort, the prospect may ask himself or herself, 'OK, I've analyzed this salesperson's proposal thoroughly. Now, do I want to adopt this service?' The fifth word is *adopt*.

Now we will convert these five words, each symbolic of a varying level of resistance, into closing techniques in which we cannot be rejected, and the prospect will tell us what they are thinking, so our timing is just right.

TIME FOR A DECISION

In review, you have gained a positive response to a FABR or the prospect has agreed that you have resolved any objections. You now are ready for your first closing technique: "Are you *aware* enough, of what we have been discussing, to decide what you want to do?"

If the prospect says no, they are not being negative toward you. You cannot be rejected with these closing techniques. A no is not a negative reaction, but instead a request for more information.

If the person says they are ready to make a decision, but have decided not to buy, then, obviously, you still have objections to resolve. Ask the prospect why he or she does not want to buy, determine if the objection is real by rephrasing the objection in question form and then use the Feel, Felt and Found technique.

INTEREST IN MAKING A DECISION

Once you have given the prospect the information they are requesting or have successfully dealt with their objections, you are ready for the second closing technique: "Have I given you enough information, that you now are *interested* in making a decision?"

Information and Objections

The buying decision is the result of achieving two primary objectives:

- Giving the prospects the information they want and
- Resolving their objections.

In other words, there are only two major reasons why prospects will not buy from you:

- They have objections or
- They need more information.

You will increase your effectiveness in closing, therefore, if you concentrate, not so much on the close, but on what you must accomplish so that the buying decision can occur automatically. Keep asking yourself, Have I given this prospect all the information they need and have I resolved all their objections?

Consider, for example, how often a salesperson may confuse a prospect by using unfamiliar terminology. Remember when you first began in the business, how many words and concepts you did not understand. Then, as you became proficient, these words became part of your normal conversation. Today, you may assume that the prospect is equally familiar with such words, even though you may sound like you are speaking in Latin. Remember always to speak in the vernacular.

Most people are reluctant to admit when they are confused by your terminology, for it is as though they are admitting ignorance. You always must put yourself in the prospect's position. Think as he or she thinks and you quickly will understand the objections that you have yet to resolve or the information you have yet to give.

Evaluating the Proposal

Assuming that you have accomplished both objectives—providing the necessary information and resolving any objections—you now are ready for your third closing technique: "Have you *evaluated* my proposal thoroughly enough, so that you now are ready to finalize your thinking?" Again, a no is a request for more infor mation, so there is no rejection. A yes is your signal that the prospect is ready to make a decision, so your timing is just right.

Analyzing the Product

Once you have given the prospect the additional information they requested or resolved any further objections, you are ready to use the fourth closing technique: "Have you *analyzed* my proposal thoroughly enough, so that you are ready to make a decision?"

Adopting the Service

Again, once you believe that you have given the prospect all the information they need and that you have resolved all their objections, then you are ready for the fifth closing technique. Simply ask, "Are you ready to *adopt* my recommendations?"

In review:

- "Are you *aware* enough of what we have been discussing to make a decision?"
- "Have I given you enough information, so that you now are *interested* in wrapping this up?"
- "Do you feel you have *evaluated* my ideas in enough detail to know what you want to do?"

- "Have you *analyzed* my proposal thoroughly enough, so that you are ready to make a decision?"
- "Are you ready to *adopt* my recommendations?"

Review the first four of these techniques. Do they seem the same? You should feel that they are, for in selling, as in tapestry, you do not want people noticing your technique. You want the threads woven together, for if a technique becomes noticeable, then it may distract the prospective customer and discredit your position.

To illustrate the important, yet subtle, differences between these five closing techniques, imagine that you are walking past a pet shop. You notice an animal in the window, but it does not really attract your attention. You may think to yourself, I am *aware* that there is something in that window.

It takes more than awareness to motivate you to go back to the window and say to yourself, 'That's very *interesting.*' It takes a greater degree of consciousness to motivate you into the pet shop and say, "I would like to *evaluate* what that is. How much does it cost and what do you feed it?" It takes a greater degree of interest for you to ask, "Can I take it home on a trial basis and *analyze* how my children react to it and how it behaves?"

It takes an even greater level of desire to motivate you to return to the seller and say, "I'd like to *adopt* the pet." "I'd like to adopt your recommendation regarding my insurance needs." Or, "I'd like to adopt your computer system."

Remember that there are many closing techniques available. They are, however, all supplements to these five techniques which eliminate rejection while giving you insight into the person's thinking, so your timing is accurate. With these five closing techniques, you will know when it is time to give more information, resolve objections or ask for a decision.

Trial Close

For example, a favorite closing technique to use before employing these five techniques is "trial close with humor." Think back to FABR. Imagine you are presenting the features, advantages and benefits of your product, and when asking for a response, the prospect is enthusiastically positive. At that point, with humor in your voice and a smile on your face, you ask, "Well, then, how about buying two?"

If the prospect says "How much would that cost?", he or she may have more money than you realized. Then, you may want to get serious and discuss a larger order.

If the prospect says, "I can hardly afford this," you are on target and should focus on selling just what you have been presenting.

If the prospect says, "I can't even afford this," you have yet to justify the cost of what you are selling. Your options are to reduce the price of the item or reduce the amount of the product that you are offering the prospect or offer a less-expensive product.

THE SELLING CYCLE

Keep in mind that, based on the complexity of your products, these five closing techniques might be spread over a long period of time.

If you are selling a relatively simple product, you may need a decision on the first contact. Otherwise, you need to move on to the next prospect, particularly when the list of potential buyers is somewhat unlimited and your commission is relatively low.

The more complex your products, the greater the commissions and the fewer your qualified prospects, the more you will need to "hang in forever" and use these closing techniques, often over a significant period of time.

For example, if you are selling mainframe computers, and you asked the prospect, "Are you aware enough of what I am offering you to make a decision?", he or she may say, "No, I need more information. I understand that you give seminars regarding your technology and the applications as they relate to my needs."

So a few weeks later, the prospect attends your seminar, and afterward you call back and ask, "Did you get all the information that you needed, so that you now are interested in making a decision?"

The prospect may reply, "I need a proposal. I am becoming more aware of how complex this really is, and I need to evaluate this system more thoroughly, so send me your recommendations with the emphasis on my needs."

You do the research, send the proposal and, on an agreed-on time, you call again, "Have you evaluated my proposal thoroughly enough, so that you are ready to wrap this up?" The prospect says,

"I want my controller to analyze your recommendations, and I must speak to one of your customers, so I can better understand a few crucial details."

You provide the necessary names of the customers who would be most ideal for your prospect to contact and then call back and ask the final question, "Are you ready to adopt the computer?"

We, as marketing people of sophisticated products, are moving people through levels of consciousness, never so quickly as to threaten them and never so slowly as to have them lose interest.

Using these techniques, you never will be rejected, for a no is only a request for more information, and your prospect will tell you when he or she is ready to make a decision, so your timing is just right.

COUNSELING AND SELLING

If you can fix the product you are marketing, you can sell it. If you cannot fix it, then rather than selling it, you need to counsel the prospect through the process.

More specifically, we need to understand that the greatest fear of rejection in selling is:

- not in prospecting, when people may react negatively toward you;
- not when dealing with objections, which you may not be able to overcome;
- not when closing and perhaps losing to the competition;
- but when the prospect buys from you and then becomes negative afterwards.

Consider the stockbroker who develops hundreds of clients in his first few years of selling during a bull market. Just as he is doing well financially, the market drops, the value of his recommendations declines dramatically and he assumes that his clients are unhappy because of all the money they have lost.

He decides, for fear of rejection from his existing clients, that he would confront less hostility if he developed new clients, so he returns to cold calling. Often the broker does not feel the same enthusiasm he did when he began in the business and, rather than prospecting again, decides to resign.

There is, however, a selling process that can resolve the problem. Rather than make recommendations which you cannot guarantee, consider the way psychologists and counselors sell ideas in their professional capacities.

They follow a four-step process:

1. Understanding the person's objectives, of what they want to accomplish;
2. Being aware of the obstacles which are preventing the person from achieving their objectives;
3. Developing a variety of solutions which might be appropriate; and
4. Deciding which solution seems most ideal and employing it.

In the example of the stockbroker, he begins by asking questions which provide a broad perspective of the prospect's needs and what they wish to accomplish: "Are you interested in an investment which is safe and secure or one that has the potential for a significant profit in the near future?"

The prospect may respond, "I'd rather gamble on investments that are exciting."

"Then how about penny stocks? We think we have found gold in the Yukon, though we have not yet begun mining. The stock seems very interesting at $1.25 a share."

The prospect responds, "I want to take chances, but I'm not crazy."

"Then let's discuss blue-chip stocks which are in growth industries."

"That is what I like."

The broker then asks, "What industries do you enjoy following?"

The prospect says, "I like airlines and the computer industry. Let's try airlines."

The broker reviews the major airlines, their strengths and difficulties. The prospect selects the airline he or she prefers and the broker asks the last question, "Do you want one thousand or two thousand shares?"

Then, if the price of the stock drops, the broker can call the client and say, "I guess *we* made a mistake. I need to meet with you to discuss whether we should stay committed to our present decision or strategize a different approach. When can we have lunch?"

This is the crucial idea: to position yourself so that you can call back if the decision goes badly. You want to make "we" decisions.

Of course, prospects often will be in varying ends of the spectrum of decision making. While some might be in the middle and prefer making the decisions with you, certain dominant prospects will want you to conduct research for them and let them make the decisions. On the other side of the spectrum are those prospects who will want you to decide for them. If you do decide for them, however, then they are equally responsible for the outcome of the investment.

In review, there are two types of products or services which you can sell. First are those products you can repair or replace if they do not function properly, such as appliances, automobiles and computers. If the customer is unhappy with the product and you can take it back, then you can feel comfortable making strong recommendations. In other words, if you can guarantee that the product will perform according to your assurances, then you can take an aggressive position.

The second type are products that cannot be fixed if they do not work, such as financial investments like stocks and bonds. If you cannot guarantee the results which you predict, nor fix it if it fails, then you should not be selling it. The way you stop selling and instead help people buy is to *know your client* and make sure the client understands the potential risks and rewards.

Use counselor selling. Guide the prospect through the decision-making process. With this involvement, you then position yourself for a long-term relationship which can culminate in repeat business, diversified products and significant results.

Think of the Hewlett-Packard advertisement, with the theme "What if. . .?" Whenever you confront any obstacles in the way to your objective, ask, "What if. . .?" and allow the power of your subconscious mind to influence your thinking.

Recently, I was asked by IBM to give a lecture in Toronto, preferably on Thursday. I was about to explain that every day was scheduled that week when I asked myself, What if. . .? and quickly my mind began to develop solutions.

Shearson Lehman was scheduled from 1:00 until 4:00 at the World Trade Center in New York. What if I started for IBM at 8:30? They wanted a two-hour presentation. I would be finished by 10:30, be at the airport by 11:10, get through customs and security in twenty minutes, make the 11:35 to La Guardia, a taxi ride at 1:10, ask Shearson Lehman to start one hour later, be at the 103rd floor by 2:00, catch the 7:00 flight to Houston, rent a car and drive for an hour.

As I fell asleep that night I thought, 'I worked for five hours, relaxed on both flights, no big deal.'

You can achieve almost any objective if you really feel the accomplishment would be worthwhile. Imaginatively develop various ways to succeed and just persevere patiently.

9

Relating to Everyone

Change can be as simple as turning your diamond to that facet of your personality that matches the person or the situation you are confronting.

Our results are based on relationships. The more complex the product we are marketing, the more we need to create relationships in which people feel comfortable with us. Because people are different, however, the relationships they prefer will vary. Consider four different types of people and the unique relationships that you need to develop to gain meaningful dialogues and the desired results with each of them.

THE ONE-TO-ONE RELATIONSHIP

Various types of relationships exist, whether in a selling environment or in any part of your life. One kind of relationship occurs when a person wants to be equal with you. This is a warm, sensitive person who wants you to be their friend. This person prefers to speak with you on a sharing basis and wants a one-to-one type of relationship.

CONTROL

The second person is aggressive and prefers a relationship in which they are in control. These people like to have others follow their instructions and enhance their positions.

THE SUBSERVIENT PERSON

The third person wants to be taken care of. This group of people is subservient and wants people to help them feel secure. They are receptive, passive and humble. They will listen to you and prefer someone who they can depend on to resolve their problems.

THE SELF-RELIANT TYPE

The fourth person does not want a relationship. They want their own space. These people do not want others telling them what to do, as control types will try to do to them. They can become irritated with friendly people who slow them down from "doing their own thing," and they get frustrated with subservient people who may want to depend on them.

Think of the kind of relationship which you prefer. Also, how effective are you in reading people, to know who you are dealing with and the type of relationships they prefer?

MOTIVATING NEEDS

If you want to sell people on your ideas, then you first must relate to them. Only then will they reciprocate. In other words, if you want people to be responsive, follow your recommendations and tell you how they feel, you must satisfy their emotional needs. What you do to create an effective relationship with one person may distract or irritate someone else.

Friendship and Acceptance

More specifically, assume that you correctly identify the prospect as a friendly person. Then think of what this person needs from you to feel comfortable. Friendly people need positive feedback, praise and recognition. The more people who like and accept this person, the happier he or she will be. If you are pleasant and conversational, this person is more likely to be receptive to your suggestions.

Dominance and Power

Aggressive, control-type people want power, and there are two types of power. First is ego power, in which the person desires status and will go into debt to acquire the symbols of affluence. Then there is money power, in which the person may become miserly to accumulate wealth. They enjoy a competitive or dominant relationship to satisfy their ego needs.

Security and Being Taken Care Of

Subservient types need security and want you to take care of them.

Solitude and Independence

The self-sufficient person wants to be independent. This person becomes irritated when people interfere with their individuality.

Imagine, for example, that you are in a very competitive situation with a primary prospect with a product line which is not within your expertise. Yet there is someone within your region who can persuasively make the presentation.

You can bring this person to your appointment and feel somewhat assured of making the sale or go on your own and take a strong chance of failing. What do self-reliant people do?

They will make the effort on their own, for to ask someone for help and succeed is, to them, a form of failure, of having to depend on someone; but to go try on their own and fail is a form of success, for they feel they were gutsy and self-reliant.

In review, think of the ways in which these types of people want you to relate to them.

The warm, sensitive person wants you to be a friend, because he or she wants to feel accepted. The control type wants to dominate you, to achieve a sense of power. Subservient people want you to take care of them and make them feel secure. The self-sufficient group wants you to leave them alone, to attain a sense of independence.

READING PEOPLE: *PETS*

Think of the ways in which you can read people, to understand how to relate to them, so they will be receptive to what you have to offer. A simple way to read people is to consider the pets that people own. People tend to choose pets that they can relate to, feel comfortable with or emulate. Pets often are reflections of the needs that motivate their owners.

More specifically, what kind of a dog do you think each of these types of people would have? A friendly person owns a poodle, for taking care of such a dog is like raising a child. They also prefer large, shaggy dogs which they can hug like collies. The favorite dog for a warm, sensitive person probably would be a cocker spaniel, which is the cutest, friendliest dog of all.

Aggressive, dominant people prefer pit bulls, Doberman pinschers and German shepherds. In fact, control types often prefer breeding Dobermans and German shepherds together to combine the most aggressive qualities of each.

Humble people, who seek security, relate to nervous dogs, such as Chihauhaus. These people prefer tiny dogs that they can hold in their hands.

Self-sufficient people do not own dogs, because they prefer animals which do not need constant affection. If this person does own a pet, it probably will be a cat.

As a way of illustrating the connection between pets and the complexity of relationships, consider the story of two brothers. One was a friendly person who criticized himself for being too sensitive and decided to become more self-sufficient. So he bought a cat that he could emulate, which became a major part of his life. His brother was a macho, beer-drinking truck driver.

Obviously, the brothers did not enjoy a good relationship, which did not concern the aggressive, dominant brother, but did upset the brother who was sensitive. In an effort to improve the relationship, while on his annual trip to Europe, he left his cat with his brother. While he was in Paris, a telegram arrived, stating, "Your cat died."

He called his brother. "OK, my cat died, but you know that my cat was my whole life. You could have broken the news to me gently, sending a telegram saying, 'Your cat is on the roof.' The next day you could say the cat fell off the roof. Then you could have sent a telegram saying the doctor is having trouble saving my cat."

His brother said, "OK, I understand."

The following year, he went to Europe and left his new cat with his brother. While he was in London, a telegram arrived: "You're cat is doing fine; the weather is wonderful. P.S. Mom is on the roof."

We need to realize that people are different and that what frustrates one person might be very different than what might irritate someone else. Before you can establish rapport you need to read the prospect, determine which type of person he or she might be and what type of relationship the prospect might prefer.

READING PROSPECTS: *THEIR OFFICES*

Imagine, for example, that you arrive for an appointment and the prospect's secretary tells you he is still in a meeting and that you should make yourself comfortable in his office. In what way does the prospect's office indicate the type of person that he or she might be?

What will you find in a friendly person's office which will symbolize their need for an equal, sharing relationship? There may be family pictures and a photograph of a cocker spaniel. You also may find hanging plants, warm colors and an emphasis on a coffee-table and seating arrangement that is conducive to social conversation.

The office of the control type probably will contain trophies and awards which were won in competitive activities, such as at a golf tournament or a marketing contest. There may be pictures of people who this person has fired. The desk will be a symbol of their need for power and the desire to be in a dominant position.

The subservient type usually will have a neat desk, with paperwork in place and possibly a calendar indicating how much time remains before retirement. The self-sufficient prospect may display unique artwork from a primitive culture as a symbol of their individuality.

People however, are complex. If you make quick assumptions, you often may miss other factors which are more important. For example, a person's office may indicate the way he or she wants associates and employees to perceive him or her. The way this person wants you to relate to them, on the other hand, may be very different.

Seating Arrangements

Another approach in reading the prospect, which might be more appropriate, is to consider the seating arrangement. The friendly person will say, "Let's forget the desk. Sit over here by the coffee table so I can see more easily what you want to show me." This person wants you to be their friend. An ideal reaction might be for you to say, "It's almost twelve o'clock. How about lunch? Would you like to bring someone along?"

The control type will sit behind their big desk, tell you where to sit and then do all the talking.

The subservient type may ask you, "Where would you prefer that I sit?" Most salespeople obviously prefer such prospects.

The self-sufficient type, while still standing, will ask, "What do you want to discuss, so I can tell you who to speak with?" This person is telling you that he or she does not want a relationship.

WHO YOU NEED TO BE

In review, the one-to-one prospect wants you to be their friend. The subservient person wants you to be their mother or father and take care of them. The self-sufficient type wants you to also be self-sufficient. He or she does not prefer pleasant, lengthy conversation. Just "net it out" and "give it to me straight."

The control-type prospect is the real challenge. Think of the type of salesperson this type would prefer. You may decide that aggressive prospects want you to be subservient and follow their instructions, and that is true. If you act subserviently, however, they also may disrespect you and may not want to deal with you. The answer may be to become a control type. This is correct, for the prospect will respect you and decide, "You are someone I can relate to." You also may irritate them, if they feel that you are trying to dominate them or "make them look bad."

The solution is to begin as a control type and gain the prospect's respect, but be very aware of the moment when he or she may seem threatened by your confidence. When that happens, make a quick and subtle transition to subservience.

In other words, with control types, do not be as hostile as they are, but be as confident; do not act so opinionated or adamant, but be as decisive and assertive. Such prospects often enjoy playing "mental racquetball" and using sarcastic humor. The balance between gaining their respect and irritating them, however, is a very delicate one. If they seem as though they are becoming negative toward you, then quickly interrupt yourself and ask a question such as, "Do my suggestions make sense to you?" or "How do you feel about these ideas?"

Think of people you know who are warm and sensitive and want you to be their friend. Think of power-oriented people who either want to control you or enjoy confrontational relationships. Think about those who are subservient and want people to take care of them, as opposed to those who "do their own thing" and are loners, perhaps to the extent that they may become antisocial.

Now, which person do you tend to be and which person do you enjoy relating to? Do any of these people frustrate you because you may have difficulty dealing with them? How effective are you in developing a relationship with each of these people, so you can gain the desired results?

BEHAVIORAL PATTERNS

Your needs determine the way you behave and your behavior is a primary factor in your success. What would you do if you had a day in which you could do whatever you wished?

Communication

The behavioral pattern of the friendly person, if he or she had a choice, is to devote their day to talking with people and socializing. Often referred to negatively as "people pleasers," they are excellent communicators, such as in:

- Relating with people to establish rapport;
- Understanding when determining needs; and
- Being helpful in developing solutions.

However, they have difficulty being persuasive, not just in business, but also in their personal lives.

Their problem is caused by a fear of rejection. As discussed before, once they develop a friendly relationship, they avoid being persuasive, such as describing reality, dealing with objections or closing, for fear they may antagonize the prospect and damage the relationship.

Persuasiveness

The aggressive, control-type person devotes the day to gaining results. Winning is very important for these people. They will even tell you that "Winning is not the most important thing. Winning is the only thing." To this extent, they will manipulate people, often just for the fun of it.

Listening Power

The humble, subservient salesperson is excellent in listening to people, following their instructions and doing what is asked of them. These people, however, have difficulty functioning on their own or taking the initiative because of feelings of insecurity.

Self-Discipline

The self-reliant salesperson does not like to take instructions nor to depend on people. They want to function on their own. They are self-disciplined, introspective and self-managing.

By now, you probably have a good idea of what type of person you are. Since most people are a combination of all four, write down all four words, friendly, control, subservient and self-sufficient, in the order in which you see yourself. In other words, decide who are you, most of all, second of all, third and least of all.

SUCCEEDING IN BUSINESS

Each of these four types of people can succeed in business, if they take on a job which plays on their strengths and does not touch their liabilities.

For example, the friendly person will function well as a social worker, teacher or counselor. They also will be successful in personnel, public-relations and staff work, where they can be supportive of other people by being sensitive to their needs and helping them.

The control type will perform well in management, particularly when the position requires making difficult decisions under pressure. They also will be successful as marine drill masters or prison guards.

The subservient person needs a job where he or she does not have to think, but merely follows instructions, such as doing factory work on an assembly line.

The self-sufficient type will be most effective as an entrepreneur in their own business. They also will function well as a research scientist working alone in a laboratory or as a hermit or a monk.

SUCCEEDING IN SELLING

Think of how effective each of these people is in selling. Actually, all can succeed if they take on selling positions that match their strengths rather than exposing their liabilities or "triggering" their fears.

The friendly salesperson will operate best in a counseling-type sales position where the competition is minimal and the primary requirement is providing information. For example, selling for a utility, such as the telephone company, historically has been a public-relations job, informing people of new telephone systems that may be ideal for their application. The telephone industry is becoming more competitive, however, and many warm, sensitive people are becoming frustrated when they are asked to be more aggressive and persistent.

The control type will perform well on straight commission and in door-to-door sales, such as selling vacuum cleaners and books. Using 13 closing techniques on an 83-year-old lady often is amusing to this type, thus the negative stereotype of people in sales.

Subservient salespeople usually will function effectively in retail selling, where they wait for people to come to them. They will follow people's requests, act passively and write the order.

Self-reliant people will serve well as manufacturers' representatives, where they work on their own and do not depend on any single company for their livelihood. They do not like to "play politics" or have authority figures tell them what to do.

Conflict and Frustration

The major frustration that you may experience, not just in business, but also in your personal life, is when the person you are does not match the person you are with, the responsibilities that you confront or the objectives you want to achieve. Then a gap will exist, between where you are and where you need to be. The greater the gap, the greater the frustration. This is why frustration can be positive for it tells you that you are out of balance, and that change is required.

Thus, if you ever become frustrated again, ask yourself three questions. First ask: "Of the four personalities, who am I that I should be frustrated at this time?"

Understandably, it is easy to become frustrated in selling when we, as well as others, expect so much of ourselves. We need to relate to everyone, deal with a variety of challenging responsibilities and meet high expectations.

Determining Your Personality

If you do not know who you are, there are three ways to determine which of the four personalities you might be.

Your Thinking

First, pay attention to how you are thinking. For example, who would you be if, when frustrated, you were thinking to yourself, 'This person is being unkind to me. I've been trying to please him and he is being insensitive to me.' Obviously, if rejection is your primary frustration, then you are in a friendly mode.

Your Feelings

If you do not understand who you are by the way you are thinking, consider how you are feeling. If a person were to decide, "I am frustrated, which means someone probably is messing with my position. Since people have difficulty handling stress, I will give them my stress, making them weaker, more dependent on me, and then I'll feel good." This person is obviously the aggressive, dominant type.

Your Behavior

If examining the way you are thinking or feeling does not give you any insight into who you are, and why you are frustrated, then watch how you are behaving. For example, how would you react if someone cut you off on the highway? The way you behave is a reflection of the person you are at that moment.

The friendly person will wave. He or she believes that the only reason a person would cut them off is because that person is in trouble.

The control type, when cut off on the road, moves into battle. Forgetting their own schedule, they "track the guy down." Now two feet in front of the person, they begin to maneuver the person off the road.

The subservient type will exit the major highway and drive the back roads to avoid any further confrontation.

The self-sufficient person is oblivious to what is happening. They are "in their own heads," disregarding other people, and frequently in meditative introspection.

What You Are Confronting

Once you have decided who you are, based on how you are thinking, feeling and behaving, you are ready to ask the second question: "What is frustrating me?" Maybe the person you are dealing with is not your kind of person. Possibly the responsibilities require an approach which is foreign to your style. Maybe the objectives you are trying to achieve are causing more stress than you believe the effort is worth.

As soon as you decide what is frustrating you, then you are ready to ask the third and last question: "Where may change occur?"

Usually, people change what they are confronting. They get divorced, quit the job or stop calling on an irritating prospect. There is an implied challenge, however, throughout this discussion, that change should occur within ourselves.

CHANGING PERSONALITY

There are three ways in which you can change your personality, so you can relate to everyone, fulfill all responsibilities and achieve all objectives. The first is the easiest to follow and the third is the most difficult.

To prepare for the first suggestion, remember that most people possess traits of all four personalities. With your boss you may be subservient, with your children you may be too dominant, with your friends you probably are friendly and when you are alone you hopefully are self-reliant.

Capitalizing on Your Complexity

Are you always the person you need to be? You might be a combination of all four personalities, but you might not be matching yourself appropriately to the situation. As an analogy, consider your personality as a diamond. Over the years, you have polished many facets of your diamond. Change can be as simple as turning your diamond to that facet of your personality which matches the person or the situation you are confronting.

For example, if you are in a self-reliant mode and in danger of short-circuiting because of all you are trying to accomplish, and someone interrupts you regarding a petty situation, you may become even more frustrated and irritable. Yet, if your child came to you with a nasty cut, then, no matter how busy you might be, you probably would stop whatever you were doing and focus all of your concern on the child's problem. Change might be as simple as turning your diamond to match the situation. Capitalize on your complexity. If you have developed every major side of your personality, then you can be whatever person you need to be to achieve your objectives.

Being Who You Must Be

The second solution is more challenging. Imagine that you are a star in a Broadway show and on a given morning you are informed that someone you feel very close to has passed away. The hours move slowly, and your depression deepens. Soon it is eight o'clock in the evening. The lights on the audience dim, the lights on the stage rise and the music begins. It is curtain call. Can you "flip a switch in your head" and suddenly "be on"? If you were to consider the primary qualities in successful people, which are missing in most others, one would be the ability to "hit a switch" within your mind and "be on."

Stress and Personality Development

If these first two solutions do not help you meet all challenges, then try the third suggestion. Consider one question: Are you the same person today that you were when you were 12 years old?

The odds are that you have matured since then. How did your personality develop?

Think back to a time when you felt uncomfortable telling jokes, speaking in front of a group or acting aggressively; and you knew a person who possessed the qualities which you needed. Maybe that person was a movie star or a visiting relative and you thought, "If I were more like this person, I may have more friends, gain more respect or have more fun."

Yet the transition was difficult because you were asking yourself to develop a quality which was not part of your self-image nor within your own imagination of how you perceived yourself. The situation was forcing you to turn your diamond to a rough, untouched side and to go "against the grain." This caused frustration which "triggered" stress. However, stress is a polishing agent. It polishes that rough side of your diamond. Then, as you gain positive feedback, you begin to see yourself as the person you need to be, until you have added a new dimension to your sense of identity. As you become more mature and better balanced, you are able to relate, more easily, to almost anyone.

READING PEOPLE: *FIRST DATES*

Now for a very different way of reading people. Is it possible that a single woman on a first date can read her date's intentions and what he is looking for in a relationship, merely by the way he orders in a restaurant?

Imagine that she arrives first and is seated. She has no clue of who he is or what he is like. When he arrives, before they have had any conversation which may give her insight into his personality, they decide to order.

If he is a warm, sensitive person, he will suggest, "I'll order what I prefer, you can order what you enjoy and then we can share." He obviously is a friendly person who is easy to get along with, and the evening will be filled with romantic conversation. Whatever happens usually will occur from spontaneous and mutual consent.

The control type will order for her and tell her what she will enjoy. This will be an evening of continuous struggle and confrontation.

The subservient person will watch what she orders, then order the same or ask her to order for him. This person feels insecure. He wants her to take control and make all the decisions.

The self-sufficient type will study the menu and then order something which is not on the menu. This will be a strange and unusual evening, during which the unpredictable may occur.

DETERMINING NEEDS

Once you have determined the type of relationship the prospect prefers and have established the appropriate rapport, you are ready for the second stage of the persuasion process—understanding the prospect's needs. Generally, we assume that the primary technique in determining needs is to ask questions. In reality, however, asking questions might be one of the least effective techniques to determine the prospect's needs.

Why would employing questioning techniques frustrate each of the four personalities and which techniques would be most appropriate?

Friendly and Conversational

Friendly prospects believe that being asked questions is too formal and structured. They prefer open-ended conversations and uninhibited sharing of ideas. This conversational approach may give us more insight into the prospect's needs than asking questions. When brainstorming, there is a far greater likelihood of uncovering applications that otherwise may have been overlooked.

Asking for Advice

The control-type prospects do not like being asked questions, for they believe that the only reason salespeople ask questions is to gather information to "set them up for the kill." If you persist in asking them questions, they may answer with inaccurate information that will distract you.

Only one question is appropriate to ask the control type: "Considering your proficiency and expertise in this area, could you tell me if there is any way in which I might be of help to you?" Then lean back and listen.

Telling the Prospect

Subservient prospects become insecure when being asked a question for three reasons. First, they do not know the answer. Second, they do not understand the question. Third, they feel that if you are asking them questions, then you do not have the answers. Thus, they think to themselves, 'We are all in trouble.'

Rather than questioning the subservient type, tell them what their needs might be. They want to believe that you are an expert and that you understand their situations. You, therefore, need to assure these people that you are an authority who is proficient within the subjects being discussed.

Conducting Research

Self-sufficient prospects do not like being asked questions because they do not respect people who depend on them. They may even tell you, "When I was in your position, I never depended on people for information, for you never can be sure of their accuracy. Ask four people on a street corner for directions and each will point in a different way. The only way to be sure is to do research. When you have met with my advisers, then send me a one-page letter outlining what you have determined."

In review:

- Uninhibited conversation with the friendly prospect will give you greater insight into all the possibilities.
- Ask the control-type prospect to tell you what their needs might be.
- Tell the subservient prospect what their needs are.
- Conduct research and then give a brief, outlined report of what you have determined to the self-reliant prospect.

READING PEOPLE: *CARS*

Another way to read people, to more effectively relate to them, is to consider the automobiles they drive. The cars we drive are reflections of our self-images or often, and more importantly, the images that we would like to have of ourselves.

Think of the type of car that friendly people would drive. They prefer station wagons or minivans for weekend picnics. In the

United States, buying an American-made car is important, because of loyalty to the country. The preferred color of warm, sensitive people is blue, though a gentle beige, optimistic white or a pleasant green also would be appropriate. If friendly people are financially successful, they still will buy less-expensive cars, to avoid causing resentment among those who are not doing so well as they are. For our one-to-one type person, therefore, the preference is a blue Chevrolet station wagon or a white Ford minivan.

The control type needs a big car to take control of the road or perhaps a small tank.

These people want comfortable sedans, so that when there are foursomes for golf or executive business lunches, they do the driving, for they have the roomiest cars. Then, when this type starts cutting people off on the road, no one can complain because it is their car.

These dominant people need to own the most expensive models and if they cannot afford them, they will buy used cars or pay on ten-year loans. For specific examples, a dominant person will drive a metallic-gold Cadillac sedan, a symbol of affluence and success. Also ego-satisfying would be a Lincoln Continental, black with red interior; a Mercedes sedan with the bronze-brown color of expensive wood paneling; or a Jaguar sedan, the color of dark burgundy.

The subservient type will drive a used Yugo.

The self-sufficient types need small sports cars, to cut in and out of traffic, so no one can slow them down, and so they can find tiny parking spaces and keep their sense of freedom. They prefer foreign cars to show their uniqueness and individuality. Their favorite color is the Lone Ranger color—silver. This person also needs a sunroof to feel as though "the sky is the limit." Therefore, for the self-reliant person, the ideal car would be a silver Porsche, with a sunroof and only one seat.

Think of how people can amuse you and also how they can frustrate you. If you are to succeed in selling, you need to find the humor in what usually has frustrated you. Make selling a game.

PRESENTING THE BENEFITS

Now apply this perspective of people to the remaining stages of the selling process. Think of the ways you need to present the benefits of your products when dealing with a friendly prospect versus a control type, a subservient person or someone who is self-sufficient.

The friendly person wants to converse with you and feel comfortable sharing their feelings.

The control type wants to feel as though you are an authority on the subject, so he or she can respect you. Your presentation should be given, however, in such a way as to enhance the prospect's position.

The subservient prospect wants you to make them feel secure. They need to believe that if anything goes wrong, you will "back them up" and resolve any possible problems.

The self-sufficient types want you to "net it out" and "give it to them straight." Keep the presentation simple and straightforward.

As a market-driven salesperson who can see the world from the prospect's viewpoint, it is your responsibility to relate to each person, based on their motivating needs. Be imaginative and use good judgment. Think of the ways you could overcome objections, close and follow up, with each of the four personalities.

OVERCOMING OBJECTIONS

Friendly people want to feel comfortable expressing their concerns. They want you to listen to them and discuss the ways in which you will resolve their apprehensions.

The control type wants to tell you the reasons for their disagreement, as well as instruct you on how to deal with the situation. If this aggressive prospect does not know how to resolve the problem, he or she will demand that you explain how the situation will be taken care of.

Subservient prospects often are inhibited in expressing their insecurities. Yet they want you to cause them to feel comfortable when telling you of their fears. They need reassurance that whatever problems develop will be resolved. Speak with confidence, therefore, when you explain the way you will take care of them.

The self-sufficient prospects will tell you what is distracting them. They expect you to be logical and concise in explaining how you will deal with the situation.

READING YOURSELF: *MUSIC*

A primary challenge in selling is managing ourselves. This requires an understanding of the person we are. As a way of understanding your personality, think of the music you enjoy.

Friendly people enjoy romantic songs of love and rejection such as the popular song "Feelings." Control types prefer marching music and the "Marine's Hymn." Subservient people enjoy the music of the 1930s—sad songs and the blues. Their most popular song is "People...who need people, are the luckiest people in the world."

Self-reliant people dislike such songs. They prefer the music of Frank Sinatra, "I did it my way."

The more you understand the parts of life which you enjoy, the more easily you will realize why you prefer certain challenges, avoid others and what you may need to do to become more effective, as in the next challenge of the selling process.

CLOSING

The friendly prospects want to believe that your recommendations are for their benefit. Thus, your suggestions should focus on your concern for helping them.

The control-type prospects want to believe that they are making their own decisions. While you may offer recommendations, you need to finish your presentation by asking, "...and what do you prefer?"

The subservient prospects want you to decide what is most appropriate for their situations. The decisions which they prefer will be the ones that resolve their apprehensions and cause them to feel secure.

The self-reliant types want you to provide them with the necessary information, so they can make their own decisions. Avoid lengthy conversations and give them the facts.

FOLLOW-UP

Remember that a sale does not end with the sale but with customer satisfaction. We need to view the selling process, not as linear with a beginning and an end, but as circular as the changing of the seasons. We plant seeds and they grow and bear fruit. Then comes a quiet time when the process does not end, but becomes dormant. Then, as in springtime, the cycle begins again. So in selling, we progress through circular patterns.

Effective follow-up does more than ensure that the customer is satisfied with his or her buying decision; more importantly, it increases the opportunity to gain additional business, such as marketing diversified products, developing repeat sales and obtaining referrals.

The friendly person wants to hear from you soon after the purchase. They want to know you care and that you are interested in them. Such people fear that the only reason salespeople are friendly is to take advantage of them, to take their money. They want you to call to resolve any doubts that they may have developed and to assure them that you are someone they still can trust.

Control types want you to follow up, but only on their terms. They will decide when you call back and who you contact. Ask them, "When should I tune in with you to make sure everything is OK?" and "Should I call you or one of your people?"

Your responsibility is to assure the success of their buying decisions. This requires that you follow up according to their instructions. Remember, when dealing with dominant decision makers, you must balance your aggressiveness, which they will respect, with subservience that convinces them that they still are in control.

Subservient clients need your follow-up to assure them that they made the right decisions and that you were honest when you told them that you always would be available if they had problems. When you call them, you may want to mention a couple more reasons why they made the correct decisions. Take them to lunch and review their situations, asking, "Is everything OK? Is there anything you are concerned about or do not understand?"

The self-sufficient type does not want your follow-up. Yet you need to call back for your own benefit to be sure the sale is solid and to explore other possibilities of what you might be able to offer. Thus, when the self-reliant person does buy from you, ask, "When should I call to make sure everything is OK or, if you don't want me bothering you, who can I contact to be sure there are no problems?"

View the sale as a success which positions you to see more clearly what your next opportunity will be.

READING PEOPLE: *SPORTS*

As a last exercise of reading people, consider sports. What do you think would be the favorite physical activity of each of these four personalities?

The friendly person prefers team sports of a noncompetitive, noncontact nature, such as volleyball and softball. They also prefer, if one team begins to win, to change sides to keep the score even.

The control type prefers team sports of a competitive, contact nature, such as football, racquetball and rugby. They also enjoy hunting in groups from helicopters.

The subservient person enjoys playing Simon Says and Follow the Leader. They would rather be a caddy in golf, a mascot in baseball or a water boy in football, than actually take the initiative. They watch bowling on television and in the Olympics they might be a javelin catcher.

The self-reliant type enjoys sports of solitude, such as long-distance running, skydiving or backpacking.

Which of these four people do you tend to be, and of the four, who do you prefer being with? What qualities could you develop which would help you relate to everyone, fulfill all responsibilities and achieve your objectives?

PART
3

Achieving Excellence

10

Developing Your Potential

See yourself not as you are but as you can become.

Think of why some people, when they fail, will decide: 'I never should have tried. I guess I will never succeed.' And others will say to themselves: 'Since I deserve to succeed, I will have to make an even greater effort.'

Also consider why some people, when they succeed, will think, 'I finally made it. I can relax and ease back.' Others may decide, 'That was just an example of how much better I can be. I'm taking this even further.'

SELF-IMAGES

This single factor, which causes such opposite reactions to both failure and success, is our self-images. More specifically, each of us has a negative and a positive self-image.

As an illustration, imagine someone who wants to achieve an objective but has failed in every previous effort. Before the person tries, their negative self-image will say, "You can't do it. Remember what happened last time? I have no idea why you keep trying when you always fail, so stop irritating yourself."

Their positive self-image will say, "You can do it. At least give it a try." You can actually hear two separate voices within yourself of a negative and positive self-image.

149

The person tries and fails again. Now the negative self-image will say, "I told you so. You didn't listen to me. There are some activities you're good at, but this is not one of them, so stop trying."

Your positive self-image will say, "At least I made the effort. And it's my right to try again."

The person tries once more and this time actually succeeds. Their negative self-image will say, "You're lucky. Feel fortunate you got as far as you did and hold your position, for if you try again, you will probably fail."

Their positive self-image will say, "I'm just getting warmed up. Here comes two in a row, and I'm going to do even better next time."

Listen to these two separate, opposite voices within your mind. Realize that, whenever you try to achieve an objective that you never have succeeded in obtaining, you may experience a conflict between you and yourself. In other words, you may have an argument between your negative and positive self-image. Conflict creates negative emotions within us, such as anxiety, stress and tension, which can cause us to feel uncomfortable.

THE NEED TO BE COMFORTABLE

Consider the needs which motivate you. Higher-level needs include the need for love, acceptance and recognition. You also have the need for achievement, identity and self-esteem. Now consider your most basic needs. More basic than security, and even more basic than life itself, is your need to be comfortable. Suicide would not occur if life itself were the most basic need. The only reason why suicide does occur is because the individual becomes so uncomfortable that he or she will sacrifice his or her own life rather than continue to experience any further discomfort.

Also realize that you do not eat when you are hungry. You eat only when you are irritated because you are hungry. For example, whenever you have had a 24-hour virus and your system is upset, the thought of eating may cause you to feel very uncomfortable. When you need to eat for your strength you do not.

In review, the reason why many people do not change is because change causes anxiety. Correspondingly, the major reason why many people will change is that, if they do not, they will experience more anxiety.

Think back to the fifth grade when it was your turn to speak in front of the class. It was your first time and your knees began to shake, your heart began to pound and perspiration formed on your forehead. You did not want to give the speech, so why did you do it?

You had no choice. Your teacher said, "If you do not give the speech, then you will take this note home to your father tonight, your mother will be here tomorrow to speak to the principal and you will spend the rest of your life in the fifth grade." She caused you so much anxiety that it was easier to give the speech and get it over with than continue thinking of what was going to happen if you did not do it.

Of course, some people will change because of praise, recognition and positive motivation. However, for many people, change occurs only when they have no choice in the matter. In other words, when they are forced into it.

Remember a time in your childhood when you had to speak in front of the class, try out for a sports team, learn how to dance or drive a car. A major part of your success today is because you were forced to change in the past. Yet when was the last time you changed, not because someone forced you to, but because you decided to change? Consider four areas of your life that you may need to change: physical, professional, social or personal.

LINES OF RESISTANCE

In every challenge of life, you will confront a line of resistance where you may decide that the possible success is not worth the irritation. You will know when you reach that line of resistance because you will experience stress. Nevertheless, while stress can break you, stress also can make you more resilient and stretch you. Gradually, a difficult challenge becomes easier and maybe, after awhile, even effortless.

Decide in which part of your life you may need to confront resistance and become more resilient. Possibly, the challenge is physical, by dropping a negative addiction or developing a positive addiction. Consider the professional part of your life, of doing better financially by disengaging a liability or stretching yourself in some way. More specifically, you may need to develop a new skill or strength. Think of your relationships with people who are important to you in which you may need to resolve a conflict or become more emotionally involved and extend yourself. Maybe, as your own best friend, you need to develop the ability to dialogue with yourself to resolve your own frustrations. Decide in which area of your life you need to develop your potential and improve your self-image.

When you challenge yourself to change, you may confront a conflict between you and yourself. More specifically, the conflict is between your negative self-image, who wants you to believe that no matter how well you are doing, you will fail in the end; and your positive self-image, who believes that regardless of the difficulty of the situation, you will succeed in the end.

As a classic illustration, consider the story of a mother who had two children. One was negative and believed that no matter how good the circumstances, in the end all would go badly. The other child was positive and felt that no matter how difficult the situation, in the end all would work out fine.

Her concern for her children, of their extreme perceptions of reality, motivated her to visit a child psychologist who specialized in such problems. The solution was simple: Place the negative child in such a wonderful situation so that the child would realize that the world sometimes can be beautiful and place the positive child in a situation so awful that the child would learn that the world often can be unpleasant.

Following the psychologist's suggestion, the mother put the negative child in a room filled with the child's favorite candy and toys. When she returned an hour later, she found her child crying. She asked, "Now what's the problem?" The child said, "If I eat the candy, it will be gone, and if I play with the toys, I may break them." She decided that this child's beliefs could not be changed, but she would try to give the positive child a sense of reality.

She put the optimistic child in a room filled with horse manure. An hour later, she returned to find the child having a great time. The child was throwing the manure in the air, leaping and jumping into it, happy and laughing. She asked, "How can you possibly enjoy yourself in a room filled with horse manure?" The child said, "There has to be a pony in here somewhere." These same two children may live within you—two opposite voices in which, whenever you try to go beyond your present performance, you may find yourself in conflict between your positive and negative self-image.

POSITIVE SELF-IMAGE

At this time, make three lists of three separate columns. The title of the first column is "Positive Self-Image." List two or three activities of your life in which you possess a positive self-image. These are challenges in which, if you were doing badly, you would continue trying. Your positive self-image, convinced that you will succeed, demands that you remain consistent and perform well.

Successful salespeople tend to level off when they reach incomes which equal their self-images and their financial needs, which are usually the same. Of course, some people's financial needs are greater than their self-images. Therefore they spend more than the incomes which their self-images financially create. A temporary solution is using credit cards and getting equity loans on their homes. The permanent conclusion often is serious financial difficulty.

Your self-image is like a thermostat which determines the room temperature. Set your thermostat for 70 degrees and at 72 degrees the air conditioner will begin to operate in summertime and cool you off. The furnace will turn off in wintertime so you do not get too hot. If the temperature drops to 68 degrees, the air conditioner will shut off in summer or the furnace will begin to work in winter.

Consciously or unconsciously, you have set your self-image for a certain income level. If your income rises above this financial level, you may cool off. Your thoughts and energy may switch to other activities, such as enjoying tennis, golf or competitive cycling; spending time with your family; or relaxing in solitude by reading books or spiritual introspection. You also may enter into an emotional period of hibernation such as sleeping late, watching television or mentally drifting.

If your income drops below the financial level set by your self-image, you may experience a new determination within your thought process and a renewal of your energy. Think of your self-image, of what you believe you are worth financially, as a thermostat. Then consider those activities within the domain of your positive self-image.

NEGATIVE SELF-IMAGE

The second column is that part of your life in which you possess a negative image of yourself. As a personal example, when playing golf, I have a negative self-image. I have to cheat to break 200. If I try repairing something in the house, when I am finished trying, the repair bill usually is bigger than it originally was. I do not enjoy the frustration, but my negative self-image convinces me that I am not mechanically inclined. When I do try, I usually fail.

Evaluate those responsibilities within your job in which you may have a negative self-image which is reducing your effectiveness. In other words, what activities do you feel uncomfortable confronting, such as conducting a seminar for prospective clients, expressing your thoughts in a written proposal or making a greater income? Think of what you do to avoid such challenges. For example, you may begin prospecting or conducting research, which makes you feel you still are being productive, or you may engage in activities which are protective, such as varying forms of procrastination.

NO SELF-IMAGE

The third and last column is a list of those areas of your life in which you never have challenged yourself. Within these activities you have yet to decide whether you are capable or not of succeeding and thus have yet to develop a negative or positive self-image.

Think of the challenges you never have confronted, such as playing the piano, downhill skiing or selling certain products. While you have yet to develop a self-image within such activities, because you have no failure or success experience, you probably will have some preconceived sense of whether or not you will succeed based on your performance in similar activities. Consider those responsibilities you have yet to confront within your business and select one that you will at least attempt to fulfill. By doing so, you can enhance your self-image and develop a momentum which can positively affect other parts of your life.

Many people avoid conflict, anxiety and discomfort by never trying those activities in which they have negative self-images. They focus only on those challenges in which they have positive self-images, feeling confident that they will succeed before they try.

If their world were to change and they had to change to survive, they may instead become obsolete. The challenge which exists in our society today is to become entrepreneurial, risk-oriented, self-disciplined and persuasive. Otherwise, disappointment and frustration may occur frequently when confronting adversity.

Recognize your two objectives when developing your potential. One is to understand yourself, such as your reaction to failure, rejection and anxiety, being aware of a conflict between your negative and positive self-image. The second is to capitalize on those techniques which can help you develop your potential, improve your self-image and gain self-esteem. In other words, know how to manage and discipline yourself until you have achieved your expectations.

These goal-achieving techniques can be used only if you have an objective that you want to reach. Therefore, decide what you want to accomplish. If you have yet to determine a goal, then decide on one now, if for no other reason but as an exercise in applying the techniques in the next few chapters.

TECHNIQUE 1: POSITIVE AFFIRMATIONS

The first technique for developing your potential is Positive Affirmations. Understanding how to use this technique requires an awareness of how your mind functions. Within your subconscious mind is your innate ability, which might be more phenomenal than you can imagine. Your subconscious mind does not think in the future, but only follows what you believe to be true in the present. It does not think in possibilities, or maybes, or shalls, or wills, but only follows what you believe to be absolutely true right now.

For example, a person who wants to stop smoking may keep saying, "I am going to stop smoking. I really am. I am going to stop smoking." Their subconscious mind will say, "OK, tell me when, because obviously you are not ready yet." When a person says, "I'm a nonsmoker," then the results can be significant. Take your objective and phrase it in positive, absolute terms and in the present tense. Your subconscious mind only follows what you consciously believe to be true. Change your self-image and you automatically change the instructions to your subconscious mind.

As an example, in a hypnosis show, the hypnotist tells a woman, "You are as straight as a board, as rigid as a piece of steel." Then she is placed between two chairs, the back of her head on one chair and her heels on the other. She is perfectly rigid. Next, a 200-pound man from the audience sits on her stomach and she does not quiver.

Then the hypnotist, with a pencil in his hand, says to her, "You cannot lift this from my hand. Try, but you cannot do it." You watch the muscles in her arm strain and the perspiration form on her forehead, but she cannot budge the pencil.

Later that evening, when the session has ended, her friends say to her, "You really were hypnotized, weren't you?" She says, "Of course not. I heard every word that was said." So they say to her, "Then try it again." She sits on the floor, with the back of her heels on one chair and the back of her head on another, but the rest of her stays on the floor. She cannot stretch herself between the chairs, but she can lift the pencil effortlessly.

Your subconscious mind only follows what you consciously believe to be true. The hypnotist, however, convinces the person that whatever he or she says is true. The person's subconscious mind, rather than responding to their own self-image, then follows the hypnotist's instructions. Therefore, if you change the instructions to your subconscious mind, you can change your results.

For example, a salesman on straight commission decides he wants to make $100,000. He says to himself, "I am going to make $100,000. I hope, if everything works out OK, and I get a few lucky breaks, I might be able to make $100,000." What are his chances of success? Consider what would happen if a hypnotist were to say, "You are going to be as straight as a board. I think if everything goes OK, and we get a few lucky breaks, you possibly may succeed." A person would not have confidence in a hypnotist who was using terminology such as, "you may possibly be able to."

Instead the hypnotist says, "You are as straight as a board, as rigid as a piece of steel." The thought is not in the future. It is now. It is not a possibility. The thought is definite.

Convert your goals into positive affirmations.

A positive affirmation may not be effective for two reasons. The first: You do not believe it. If your suggestion were, "I am a $100,000-a-year producer," but that amount was more than you believed to be possible, then the affirmation may only increase your frustration. The solution is to modify the affirmation to a level which you can accept, such as, "I am a $60,000-a-year producer." Then, as you reach $60,000, you can increase the amount based on what you believe is reasonable.

The second reason why a positive affirmation may not help you succeed, even when your goal seems reasonable, is if you cannot deal effectively with the failure and rejection encountered en route to fulfilling your expectations.

A way of resolving this problem is to create a positive affirmation which helps you overcome or capitalize on your fear of rejection. Consider the following choices or develop your own:

I reject rejection.	I need 30 rejections before lunch.
I love rejection.	Rejection makes me more resilient.
Rejection turns me on.	My success is a result of the rejection I experience.
Rejection amuses me.	Rejection stimulates me.

The Negative Voice

Think of why your negative self-image does not want you to succeed. Also, consider why this negative voice creates terrible thoughts within your mind, such as when you want to try and it says, "Why bother? This is not your thing in life." Then, when you fail and feel discouraged, it "kicks you while you're down" and says "I told you so!" When you finally succeed, this negative voice tries to take away your satisfaction by saying, "One moment, that was luck." Why does your negative self-image want you to fail?

Many people believe that our negative self-image is trying to protect us from failure, rejection and anxiety. Instead, consider our negative self-image as a separate person who lives within us, who has a fear of dying and will do whatever is required to protect its position, even though it may destroy us in the process.

The kamikaze flyer illustrates this concept. The kamikaze flyer must die to be consistent with his self-image and to feel comfortable. Conversely, if he does not die, he will deny his own sense of identity and will feel quite uncomfortable.

People do not always do what is for their benefit, but what is consistent with their own self-images. In other words, people would rather be self-destructive than deny their own sense of identity.

Why do people continue smoking, even when they know it is dangerous and self-destructive? Why, in business, do people persevere until they reach a certain level of success, then never go any further? Having negative self-images might be the same reason why people, when falling in love, have a need to destroy the relationship.

Is there any part of your life in which your behavior is consistent with your sense of identity, though also self-defeating?

TECHNIQUE 2: DESCRIPTIVE TECHNIQUE

The next technique for managing yourself is the Descriptive technique, in which you describe the person that you need to be if you are to achieve your objective. When using this technique to gain financial success, you need to think of how much money you want to make during the next 12 months and what that would be per week. For example, you may decide to make $100,000, which would be $2,000 a week.

Now imagine that you have decided to retire from selling, but you also want to keep your job. You realize that a magical way to do both would be to hire someone who looks and talks just like you and pay this person $2,000 a week out of your own pocket.

If you were to pay a person $2,000 a week, out of your own pocket, what would you expect this person to do every day?

Answer the question descriptively.

More specifically, how many calls would you expect this person to make each day, how many appointments would they have to set up each week and what level of prospect or quality of business would they pursue? Also, what kind of image would they project?

For example, imagine you are a manager and you are interviewing someone for a sales position. You ask the person, "How do you deal with stress?", and the person says:

The same as most people. When I awake in the morning, the thought of work frustrates me, so I fall back to sleep. When I awake again, I am behind schedule and, with no time for breakfast, I drink a cup of coffee. If I had moved out of bed quickly, I could have avoided the rush-hour traffic, but now I'm caught in bumper-to-bumper traffic, so I start cutting people off, just to deal with the irritation. When I arrive at work, I may challenge an associate to bet on this weekend's sporting event, to get into a competitive spirit before selling. At twelve o'clock, I'm too far behind schedule for lunch, because of my late start, so I'll eat a few candy bars to keep myself moving. Late in the afternoon, I start losing energy so I take this little pill, a stimulant, which gets me up again. By five o'clock, when I think of rush-hour traffic, I become so frustrated that the only solution is to avoid the traffic and have a few drinks. When I arrive home, I really eat, for I have had very little food during the day. Then I watch television and, if the television doesn't put me to sleep, I take this little pill that knocks me out. The next morning, when the alarm goes off, I am still groggy from the alcohol, food, television and sleeping pill, so I fall back to sleep. Then I realize I am late for work, so after a quick cup of coffee, cutting people off on the road, another bet, some candy bars and a couple of stimulants, I'm back in gear.

If you were paying someone only $200 a week, you may hire this person, with the idea that they might mature and develop healthier, more creative and productive ways of dealing with stress. However, for $2,000 a week, you would expect this person to develop a strenuous exercise program, channel the anxiety into job activities, ask for advice or meditate.

Are you doing each day what you would expect someone else to do each day? If you are not, then evaluate the only two reasons why a person may not achieve their objectives. The first: they possess negative self-images. In other words, the person does not think that they are worthy of the success. Second: The person is oversensitive to rejection.

Correspondingly, you will find two qualities in successful people. First: They believe they deserve to succeed. They possess good self-images. Second: Like raindrops off a duck's feathers, they can capitalize on rejection and negative feedback.

The purpose of the Descriptive technique is to sell you on the idea that you are not a salesperson but a manager who has hired someone who looks and talks just like you. Understand and capitalize on the duality of your own personality. First is a person who lives within you who is a child of emotions and feelings. This person easily can get excited about attending a sporting event, making a sale or falling in love. This part of your personality is also the source of your humanness, your ego and your vulnerabilities. The other person within you is objective, emotionally detached and brilliant.

You need to allow your ego to do the selling, with emotion, enthusiasm and feelings. If you start taking the negative feedback too personally and become disappointed, however, then disengage your humanness, become emotionally detached and allow your objective self to guide you through the challenges. Manage yourself through the process.

Determining Your Self-Image

When developing your potential, you need to understand how your negative and positive self-images influence you. You can determine whether your self-image is negative or positive, regardless of whether the experience is one of failure or success.

As an analogy, imagine you have a son named Johnny. You are teaching your son to jump off a diving board. Johnny has a negative self-image. He does not believe he can do it. He tries and lands on his stomach. As he gets out of the water he says, "I told you I couldn't do it. Why did you force me into it? I'm not ready for this. Can I do my homework now?" Thus, if Johnny has a negative self-image and he fails, he will use his defeat as an excuse to avoid any further effort.

If Johnny has a positive self-image and he fails, however, he will say, "I'll try again. Hold your suggestions, because that wasn't too bad for the first try, was it? I made it into the water, didn't I?" If Johnny has a positive self-image, then he will battle with failure. He will not accept defeat.

If Johnny has a negative self-image, yet somehow succeeds, in his mind he will say, 'How did that happen? I must have been lucky.' But he will not tell that to you for fear that you will say, "Then let's do it again and prove that you are not lucky." So Johnny will say to you, "Is that good enough? Can I do my homework now?" He will use the success as an excuse to back off and not try again.

Yet if Johnny has a positive self-image and he succeeds, he will say, "What's next, the swan dive or the jackknife? I'm ready for the next challenge." He will capitalize on his success and be ready to do even better.

From now on, whether in failure or success, you will have a way to determine who controls your thinking, your positive or negative self-image. Yet, the more you appreciate your potential, the less likely you will back off when you fail, but will battle with those experiences which were less than what you expected. Also, the stronger your self-image, the less likely you will level off when you succeed, but rather will capitalize on the success.

The value in succeeding is not so much for the satisfaction you gain but to see more clearly what your next challenge might be.

You need to be aware of the relationship between your expectations and your self-image. A person who raises their self-image to the level of their expectations will be satisfied. Such success creates the danger of boredom, however, unless the person takes on a new challenge and continues to grow. By raising your expectations beyond your self-image, you create a desire to improve and exceed your present performance.

Along with your negative and positive self-image, you need to recognize another voice within your mind, which is the voice of discomfort. This voice will work for or against you, depending on who controls your thinking, your negative or positive self-image. If you possess a negative self-image and you experience anxiety, your voice of discomfort may cause you to decide, "This goal that I am trying to achieve is not worth the effort." Correspondingly, the stronger your self-image, the greater the chance that your voice of discomfort will help you to succeed by deciding, "No pain, no gain."

In other words, if the more you suffer, the stronger you become, then suffering is only part of the process of becoming more resilient and eventually successful. Obviously, the more you appreciate your potential, of how good you are, the less you will accept failure, but will battle with it, and the less likely you will level off when you succeed, but will capitalize and go further.

Appreciating Your Potential

When you see an acorn, what do you see? Do you see the acorn or what the acorn can become, the great oak tree? Equally, when you look at yourself, what do you see? Do you see yourself as you are or as you can become?

Grandma Moses, at 76 years old, never had painted in her life. If she had seen herself as she was, a little old lady, she may not have been starting any new hobbies. Yet 25 years later, at the age of 101, she was a famous international artist.

Consider the true story of Kentucky Fried Chicken and Colonel Sanders, who, during the 1930s, started his own business, a gas station. With every dollar he could save, he built a small restaurant behind his gas station to feed the truck drivers and, by 1955, at the age of 65, he was worth $140,000. Then the state built a major road seven miles away. Almost overnight, with the traffic diverted, he was bankrupt and collecting Social Security.

Yet he did not see himself as a bankrupt old man, but as a self-reliant person. He took his recipe for fried chicken and drove across the country, cooking the chicken in the back of his car, trying to convince restaurant people to taste his chicken and agree with him that, because of his 11 herbs and spices, they should pay him a percentage of what they sold in chicken.

Imagine that you own a restaurant, and it is the busiest time of your day, when a white-haired old man enters with a cane, a white suit and a beard and says to you, "I have this chicken I just cooked in the back of my car. I would like you to taste a leg or a thigh and agree with me that, because of my 11 herbs and spices, it's worth a percentage of what you sell in chicken." You probably would not have been too willing to give his chicken a chance. Three years later, at 68 years of age, Colonel Sanders had two restaurants supplementing his Social Security benefits.

Seven years later, at 75, however, he was worth $15 million. When he died, at 90, he was a multimillionaire, and he deserved his success, for when he was 65 years old, he did not see himself as he was, a bankrupt old man. Instead, he saw himself in the future and decided, "That's where I deserve to be." When you decide what you deserve in life, then you understand the value of stress. You need to see yourself not as you are, but as you can become.

TECHNIQUE 3: ACCEPTANCE SPAN

The third technique for achieving your goals is Acceptance Span. This technique is based on three words. The first word is *change.* Our economic environment is changing rapidly and we need the ability to change with it. Not that many years ago, and throughout history, people did not need to change. We were hunters, farmers or factory workers, and we devoted our working lives to one specialized area.

Today people have to change. They change occupations and often have no choice but to change the way they function. New technology demands new skills. We need to capitalize on a global economy which requires more expansive thinking. Many people do not like the word "change." It sounds as though "I may become someone that I am not." If the word causes you to feel uncomfortable, then consider a more gentle word such as "growing."

Regardless of which word you use, it is so important that we are able to grow that it is not that important how much we change, so long as we at least *begin*. This is the second word. You have to start somewhere. You may be familiar with the classic Chinese proverb:

"A journey of a thousand miles begins with a single step."

For example, you are walking along a street in a major city and see workers constructing a 70-story building. They begin the construction by digging down to prepare a solid foundation. If you return six months later, the crew is working at eye level. In another three months, you may see a magnificent structure. This symbolizes our lives. If you are to succeed, you have to start somewhere. Very often, that requires digging down within yourself to create a solid foundation. Otherwise, you may feel as though you are walking on quicksand.

Deciding where to begin is determined by the third and last word, what you can *believe*. What can you *believe* to *begin* to *change?* You usually can achieve whatever you want in life, as long as you break down your challenge into a stepping-stone pattern. Stretch yourself, without burning out. When you take steps toward your target, do not take such big steps so that if you fall, you do not crash, but only trip.

For example, the year was 1969, and I was giving a four-day seminar to Coldwell Banker, a residential real estate firm. These people had been selling for three months, without obtaining a single sale or listing, so I knew they were having difficulties. At the beginning of the program, I presented two concepts—that if we are to succeed we needed:

- The ego resiliency to capitalize on failure, rejection and anxiety and
- A strong positive self-image.

Then each salesperson was asked what objectives he or she had for each day. I asked one man, "Bill, how many cold calls do you make in a day?" He said, "Art, my goal is 20 cold calls per day." I asked, "Bill, how many do you make?" He said, "Art, I don't make any."

I asked, "Bill, if your goal is 20 cold calls per day, then what is your problem?" He said, "Before having heard your ideas, I would have told you that I'm lazy and disorganized. But now I realize that I cannot see myself being rejected 20 times a day."

So I asked him, "How's 15 a day?", and he said, "I can't imagine 15 rejections a day."

"How would you feel about ten a day?" and he said, "I can't see myself being turned down ten times a day."

"How's five a day?" and he said, "Art, isn't five too little?" I said, "Obviously, Bill, five sounds reasonable to you, so make five calls a day."

His company convinced him that if he did not make 20 telephone calls a day, he would not succeed. Since he could not make 20 calls per day, he was not making any. This is a classic problem for many of us.

More than three years later, the same company asked me to speak at a breakfast meeting in July for those people who were on target for their million-dollar club. Bill was at that meeting. We nostalgically discussed our conversation of three years earlier, of what we had discovered he could *believe* to *begin* to *change*.

If we cannot succeed in a given day, we often do not try. For example, people who want to lose weight often will decide, "I'm going to lose 20 pounds. In fact, I'm going to lose 20 pounds today! In fact, if I don't lose 20 pounds today, to hell with the whole thing!"

Sometimes, achieving your objectives requires being satisfied with small successes while being stimulated to reach the next stepping-stone. Be patient with yourself and enjoy the incremental success. For example, if you want to get into shape by jogging, can you see yourself jogging a mile every day? If not, then how about a half mile a day? How about around the block once easy? How about jogging down to the bar and walking back? You can achieve almost any objective if you just break down the challenge into a step at a time. Stretch yourself without burning yourself out. What is your span of acceptance? How much can you *believe* to *begin* to *change?*

The Touchstone

Many years ago, a man was walking on the beach. He came upon a tattered book and read about a touchstone which was a smooth rock. The book explained that if he found this touchstone, all that he would ever want would be his. In the last pages he read that he could find the touchstone on a unique beach and that it would be distinguished from all the other stones for they would be cold, while the touchstone would be warm.

He found the beach and, to find the touchstone, he began to pick up stones. They were cold and he would throw them into the ocean, so he would not come across the same stone again. For days and weeks, he picked up stones, would feel them, they were cold and he would throw them into the water. Then, one day, he picked up a stone, it was warm and he threw it into the water.

Often, in our lives, we hear ideas and people give us suggestions. We try them, they often do not work, so we throw them away. Sometimes we become so conditioned to throwing ideas away, that if we suddenly found one idea which was right for us, we may automatically throw it away. As you evaluate these thoughts and allow them to stimulate your thinking, touch each one of them, decide which are warm to your touch and then capitalize on them.

11

The Value of Stress

The more you appreciate your potential, the less you will accept failure, but do battle with it, and the less likely you will level off when you succeed, but capitalize and go further.

You probably have been to a circus where you visited a sideshow with distorted mirrors. You looked into these mirrors and you laughed. You know the mirrors are lying to you because at home you have a clear mirror which reflects exactly what you look like. These distorted mirrors at the circus, therefore, cannot lie to you.

When you talk to people and they are negative to you, do you laugh? Too often we cry or become depressed. We become oversensitive and take negative feedback personally. The reason why we are vulnerable is because, while we have created mirrors which give us clear images of ourselves physically, we have not yet developed mirrors of ourselves psychologically.

Yet we need to discover who we are if we are to gain self-esteem. One way to gain a sense of who we are is to look into the eyes of people. They reflect back to us, but their reflections are not clear images of ourselves. People are mirrors of us. Unfortunately, they are distorted mirrors. Some people may praise us when we do badly, when their criticism might be more to our benefit, to help us do better. Some people may criticize us when we do well because they resent us; often this makes us adapt and conform to their standards, rather than develop our own potential. We want their criticism if we do badly, for their negative feedback helps us to make changes in our course of direction. Also, we want positive feedback when we are doing well, rather than be resented for our success.

Most importantly, we need to create feedback within ourselves through internal dialogue between our objective selves and our self-images. We need to introspect, to discover who we are, instead of depending on the reaction of others for our sense of identity when they may be only distorted mirrors of us.

TECHNIQUE 4: COMMITMENT TO OTHERS

Another technique to develop your potential and reduce or eliminate your negative self-image is Commitment to Others. This is one of the strongest techniques for achieving goals. This technique takes your fear of rejection and makes it work for you. When you commit yourself to someone, you create an obligation that often forces you to follow through.

As a personal example, many years ago, I wanted to improve my long-distance running. However, I could not awake early enough to run in the morning. Then, when I returned home at night from selling for IBM, it was often too late to run. My problem, more specifically, began in 1958 when I was in the Army. I had the top bunk. At 4:30 A.M. when the sarge walked in and yelled, "Everyone up!", the light above my bunk would temporarily blind me. I would shave with my eyes closed. When I left the Army, I had more than a goal, but an obsession, which was to sleep late the rest of my life.

I had a friend by the name of Doug Clark, an ex-boxer from Buffalo. Doug told me he was running five miles at 6:30 each morning around the Rose Bowl. I said "Doug, I'll meet you tomorrow morning." The next morning at six o'clock, when the alarm clock went off, I had a half an hour to meet him. Think of how you feel at six o'clock in the morning, when turning off an alarm clock is an effort. The thought of actually running is beyond the imagination. Besides, it was cold and dark at that time of the year, so I began to fall back to sleep. Then I realized that Doug would think, 'Mortell did not keep his promise.' I could not have Doug think that of me, so I forced myself out of bed. It was as awful as I thought it would be and I wondered why I was putting myself through such discomfort. Yet within five days, I noticed how beautiful the color of the sky is at sunrise and how clear the air. I have come to enjoy sunrises ever since. I never would have come to enjoy this part of my life if it were not for having committed myself to a friend. The promise creates the self-discipline.

Decide how much money you want to earn during the next 12 months. Then decide how many new accounts you will need to reach your financial objective, such as 100 additional accounts, or two a week. If you need to make 100 cold calls to gain one new client, which is 200 prospecting calls for two new customers each week, then you will need to experience 198 rejections a week, or 40 a day.

Compare 198 rejections to rejection from your manager. You probably are more concerned with how your manager feels about you, than what 198 strangers think. Thus, commit yourself to your manager, saying, "Boss, on Friday afternoon, before I leave for the weekend, I will have been rejected two hundred times, because if I can experience that much rejection each week I should reach my financial target."

Most likely, if you determine on a Thursday afternoon that you received only 90 rejections for the week, you probably will be prospecting through the rush-hour period, working late to prepare your cold calls for the following day and staying in positive momentum throughout Friday until you have fulfilled the obligation that you created.

At this time, make a decision:

- What you want to achieve, such as getting in shape or making quota;
- What activities will assure your success, such as jogging on a high-school track or making at least 40 cold calls a day; and
- Who you will commit yourself to, such as promising a friend you will meet at sunrise for a running workout or obligating yourself to your manager that you will make 200 cold-call conversations in a week.

Breaking Mental Barriers

Many years ago, people believed the four-minute mile could not be broken. The record was 4:02. Many believed that if a runner broke the four-minute mile, he literally could die, for many thought it was physically impossible.

It was May 6, 1954, and it had rained that day. The track was still wet and it was windy. Roger Bannister, however, decided to make the effort. He explained in advance, "My attempt this afternoon is not to break a physical barrier but a mental barrier," and that afternoon he ran 3:59. John Landy, who consistently had run the best times, but could not break 4:02, a few weeks later rather effortlessly ran 3:58. Three months later, in the same race, eight men broke the four-minute mile. Most recently, Steve Cram ran 3:46.

Your obstacles are psychological barriers and your challenge is to break them. Think of the mental barriers which might be preventing you from developing your potential. Is there, within your mind, a negative self-image which is blocking you from achieving your own expectations?

TECHNIQUE 5: COMPETITION

Consider, as a way of becoming a laser beam and achieving your objectives, the next technique for self-discipline, which is entitled Competition. This technique brings out the best in some people. You probably know people who always are moving along at a steady pace. Yet in a contest they suddenly become magnificent. Challenge someone to compete with you to achieve the same objective you are trying to reach.

Recently, in my competitive running, I would run six miles at a 7:30 pace. If a friend was with me, we often would run 6:30 per mile. In a 10K race, I would run 5:30 per mile, and these fast miles were the easiest.

Competition causes the stress to become a stimulating experience as it numbs the pain, focuses the mind and raises the energy. Whether running races, losing weight or increasing your income, you need to convert the challenge into a contest. Preferably, the person you challenge should be doing better than you so you are forced to stretch yourself, but not so far beyond your present performance to cause too much frustration. Competition can bring out the best in you.

As a salesperson, decide in which of your responsibilities you need to stretch yourself. Possibly, your immediate objective would be prospecting for new accounts, selling a particular product or increasing your income. Select a salesperson in your company who is doing better than you, but is within your reach. Then challenge this person to a one-month contest. Whoever loses pays for dinner, but the restaurant should not be too expensive. You want the competition to be somewhat friendly.

TECHNIQUE 6: EMULATION

The sixth goal-achieving technique which can assure your success is Emulation. The idea is to identify with someone who has what you need. Many people may feel that this suggestion is offensive. They often will say, "I don't copy people. I'm my own person. I don't deny my own identity." You have to be talented, however, to copy someone who is successful. Once you have mastered their approach, then you can modify it to your own personality.

Not that many years ago in the United States, we criticized the Japanese for copying us. We no longer can be critical when, in certain industries, the Japanese have far surpassed us.

More specifically, the next time you are depressed, think of someone who is successful and invite this person to breakfast or lunch. Then ask, "Were you always successful? If so, what happened in your past that you are doing so well today? When you are depressed, how do you pull yourself out of it? What do you think about when you fail? How do you react when you are rejected? How do you handle stress? How have you developed your potential?" Then, for a certain period, emulate this person. We need role models in our lives. Once you are succeeding, then integrate the quality into your own self-image.

Imagine that you are a manager and could select any actor or actress in Hollywood to sell for you. Decide who you would want. Consider Clint Eastwood: "Make my day." Think of Jack Nicholson who would be amused by difficult times and stimulated by rejection, rather than becoming depressed. Then, for a certain time period, practice his or her style and play the role.

Decide what type of salesperson causes you to feel comfortable, perhaps by the way they speak with you on the telephone. Consider the combination of qualities which they may balance together, such as being friendly, enthusiastic and confident. Then consider who you know who has those qualities and emulate this person. If the person you are is not helping you achieve your objectives, then be the person you need to be.

Negative Conditioning

Think of the conditioning in your past that causes you to believe what you can or cannot do. When you decide what you cannot do, this belief crystallizes into a negative self-image which may prevent you from developing your potential. For example, a baby elephant is exuberant and wants to run, so it is chained to a stake. The elephant tries to pull the stake out of the ground, but it physically cannot succeed.

The elephant now grows into a powerful adult animal and is able to effortlessly pull the stake out of the ground. It goes to the end of the chain. It struggles, but it fails. The elephant has the ability to succeed, but it has been conditioned to believe it cannot.

Consider those parts of your life in which you have been conditioned to believe you cannot succeed. The result is a negative self-image which can prevent you from developing your potential. Think of those limitations which might prevent you from reaching your expectations. Decide what you might do to break through your own barriers.

TECHNIQUE 7: LEADERSHIP

If you ever feel as though your world is elusive, your life is lacking structure and you are losing control, then think of monkey bars. Children enjoy playing on monkey bars, lifting themselves up and controlling their lives. Another handle or technique that can create structure in your life is Leadership. Select someone who has less seniority than you or is not doing as well as you are. This person needs help in an area in which you already are proficient, but you are not being consistent. Consider the benefits you will gain when you help someone to succeed.

First, when instructing someone, you are reminding yourself of what you should be doing. For example, you may quickly forget the ideas in this book. If, however, you were to discuss these ideas with someone, such as a friend or an associate, who could benefit from this material then, as you hear yourself expressing these thoughts, they will crystallize within your own mind and more easily become part of your philosophy. Provide your own examples and use the ideas in this book to stimulate your thinking. As you motivate someone, you also develop the ability to be your own motivator. Help people to accomplish what you need to achieve. When you offer suggestions, you reinforce your own noble aspirations.

Another benefit of Leadership occurs when the other person follows your suggestions. If you have yet to follow your own advice, then the other person's success may embarrass you into taking action. Also, helping someone else is good for your self-image.

Decide in which part of the job you are not being consistent. Possibly prospecting is easy for you, but you have not been psyched to making calls. Then invite a new person to join you on your calls, whether listening while you are on the telephone or traveling with you.

Having someone watch you while you are prospecting, making presentations or trying for the buying decision can help you stay productive. Giving advice while the other person is making the effort can sharpen your skills. Being a teacher will enhance your proficiency.

Conditioning and Patterns

Think of the conditioning which creates the behavioral patterns of your life. As an illustration, a barracuda and a mackerel were placed in the same pool of water. Now barracuda just loves to eat mackerel, but the barracuda does not know that in between it and the mackerel is a thick piece of glass. The barracuda attacks but slams into the glass. The barracuda has no idea what hit it, so it turns around and tries again, and "wham," into the glass. After awhile, the barracuda gets a headache just looking at the mackerel. Then the glass is removed from the water, the mackerel swims by and the barracuda keeps its distance, for it has been conditioned to what it cannot do.

We have been conditioned in very much the same way, of what we can or cannot do. Evaluate the conditioning of your own life, as well as the origins of your limitations, and the way a negative image may inhibit you from developing your potential.

TECHNIQUE 8: BUDDY SYSTEM

The eighth technique for managing yourself is the Buddy System. Select someone with whom you can meet once a week, for lunch or breakfast, to share feelings and exchange ideas. Women are comfortable in support groups and networking. They discuss their successes, express their disappointments and offer suggestions.

Many men tend to avoid this technique, for they feel it is not "macho" to rely on someone. The technique, however, can help you stay on track. You can sell door-to-door together. In physical conditioning, find someone to work out with, not to be competitive, but to relate to and share the same challenge. Having a friend involved with you can keep you on a schedule.

Throughout the selling process, you have a constant need to manage yourself. One of the reasons why selling is so difficult is that a large percentage of people are unable to function effectively in an unstructured environment. Therefore, to succeed in selling often requires the ability to create structure, so we can keep ourselves on target.

Think of children who live in a world which seems so big and makes them feel insecure, and how they enjoy playing on monkey bars. They want something to hang onto and feel on top of the world. Likewise, we need to create handles so that when we are in trouble, we can pull ourselves up and take control of our lives.

In December of 1966, I was frustrated that I would not make my quota for the year with IBM. With only a few business days left in the month, one of my associates explained the approach he had used to gain a significant order in which he emphasized tax-depreciation benefits.

Using the same strategy, I made the presentation and the sale; I never would have made my quota without the success of someone else stimulating my thinking.

When prospecting with your buddy, take turns on each call. Critique each other. Offer advice. Keep each other motivated.

Being Consistent

You do not have a single self-image, but several self-images. You have images of yourself, of what you believe you can do, and images of yourself, of what you feel is not within your ability. However, of all the images you have of yourself, one image must be strong and positive, and that is seeing yourself as someone who can change.

If you see yourself as a person who can change, then you can eliminate any negative self-image which might prevent you from developing your potential. If people possess negative self-images regarding their ability to change, then when the world is in transition, they may find themselves becoming obsolete. You need to see yourself as someone who can adapt. You do not want to conform but rather capitalize on the opportunities within a changing environment.

Your ability to change is actually a by-product of another part of your self-image, which is your ability to discipline yourself. If you can discipline yourself, you can change. Thus, change becomes a result of self-discipline.

Yet the ability to discipline yourself is based on an even more basic attribute and that is being consistent. If you are able to be consistent, then you automatically will be disciplined, and you will be able to change. People will tell you, "I can change. I once lost 20 pounds, but I regained 25." A salesperson may explain to you, "I have no problem making cold calls. Once I won a contest and went to Hawaii, but when I returned, I never got back into prospecting."

People can change. The challenge is to be consistent. Consistency creates self-discipline. Decide in which part of your life you will be consistent, such as running a mile a day, reading ten pages of a book, meditating, practicing the piano, doing 100 sit-ups or prospecting each day. By being consistent, you convince yourself, "If I can do this, I can do anything."

TECHNIQUE 9: SELF-COMPETITION

We previously have discussed Self-Competition as a technique to keep ourselves motivated when prospecting. While competing with ourselves can keep us disciplined to remain consistent, the technique also can help us achieve any objective.

For example, if you want to strengthen your cardiovascular system, then read one of Dr. Kenneth Cooper's books on aerobics and let him sell you on how crucial it is to empty the reservoir of stress each day through exercise. You need to burn the anxiety out of your system while gaining a sense of achievement.

His approach employs self-competition in which you take a 12-minute test to determine what kind of shape you are in by walking or running. The further you go, the better the shape you are in. Next, decide what sport you prefer and, based on the shape that you are in, the book tells you which exercise program has been designed for you. Then score yourself each week and compete with yourself.

In selling, we use the same technique. Think of the three primary activities in selling which will be referred to as *funnel, filter* and *focus*. First is prospecting in which everyone you contact seems to go into a *funnel*. Then there is the *filtering* process—qualifying, presenting solutions and gaining a reaction. In the third stage, you *focus* on resolving any conflicts, overcoming objections and closing.

In this approach, each prospecting effort is one point, filtering is a three-point play and the activity of focusing is worth five points.

Your concern is not so much with how many points you score in a day, but that you outscore what you did yesterday by one point. Who do you compete with? You compete with yourself.

Regardless of what you want to achieve, play the game of Self-Competition. Through this technique, you can lose weight, develop a strenuous exercise program or become more effective in your job. Convert your objective into a point system by placing a value on whatever you do, and challenge yourself to score as many points as you can in a day.

Remember the word "momentum." It is one of the most powerful forces in your life. It is energy in continuous movement. You can create momentum by competing with yourself and beating yesterday's score by at least one point.

You need to manage yourself in three areas of your life: how you *think, feel* and *behave*. If you manage the way you think, then automatically, regardless of what happens to you, you will feel positive. If you think negatively or become pessimistic, however, then you may become depressed. Yet if you manage the negative feelings that cause depression, then you can burn the anxiety out of your system in some form of achievement. You can exercise, work harder, counsel with someone or develop an avocation within solitude. If, however, you do not manage the way you think, and you are pessimistic, and you do not manage the way you feel, causing you to tumble frequently into a down cycle, then you still have one last chance. You need to manage the way you behave.

Though you may think negatively and feel badly, you still can function as you should. You still can play the role. Self-competition can disengage you from your own vulnerabilities. Just compete with yourself. Merely score one more point than you did yesterday, so that regardless of how you think or feel, you behave the way you must. As you gain the desired results, you will think positively and feel good.

Being a Laser Beam

A laser beam has two qualities that you want. One is power and the other is precision. A laser beam and the light that you are using at this time are the same. They both are photon or light energy. Yet, three words symbolize the difference between the light that you are experiencing right now and a laser beam. These three words create both the power and the precision.

The first word is *intensity*. If you want to become a laser beam, and be able to cut through your obstacles with precision and power, then you first need to possess intense energy. This energy comes from your own expectations. The more you expect of yourself, the greater your energy will be.

The second word is *concentrated*. The energy, more than being intense, also must be concentrated. In other words, the energy must be brought together into a single force. You then have the first two factors for becoming a laser beam.

The third word is *focus*. You must decide on a target at which you will focus your energy. You need to have positive obsessions so you are setting goals which are meaningful to you. Therefore, answer three questions:

- How much do I expect of myself?
- Is my energy concentrated?
- Do I have positive obsessions in which to focus my energy?

While our expectations determine how successful we need to be to respect ourselves, our values determine our obsessions, of what we need to achieve to feel successful.

We need obsessions in life. Mozart was obsessed with writing music, and a horse needs to run with the wind. When we have obsessions, then stress becomes meaningful.

There are four obsessions which you need in life. One is physical, for within almost every one of us is an obsession to experience the exhilaration of a physical effort which can keep us in shape. Using exercise to relieve stress and become more creative is a primary factor in our success in selling.

When your work becomes an avocation, then the stress of the job becomes as stimulating as your favorite sport. If this is not true for you, then keep experimenting with various activities until you find those challenges which you enjoy so much that the job becomes a game. Think of the percentage of your life which you devote to work and how much more satisfying your life will be if you find within your work a part which is so meaningful that your job becomes an obsession.

Falling in love is a positive obsession. The more in love you are with someone, the more easily you can deal with the conflicts that often occur.

The last obsession is an activity that you do without people and not for money or exercise. People who have yet to find a challenge that they can enjoy with themselves usually will have difficulty being alone. Become your own friend by finding an obsession, such as reading, meditation or a spiritual process, which is so satisfying that you look forward to your time by yourself each day.

Each of these obsessions can enhance the other and help you create balance in your life. Otherwise, as a laser beam, you may do more than hit the target, but destroy it.

Richard Nixon was so obsessed with power that he did more than he needed to do and destroyed what he had achieved. Famous entertainers have gained wealth and adulation, but without the necessary balance, they often experience depression and are vulnerable to suicide.

You need to manage yourself when you take on the challenge of selling. Yet managing yourself is spontaneous when the obsessions are so satisfying that the stress is stimulating and meaningful.

Also, while your high expectations can cause intense energy, your energy may not be concentrated. For instance, have you ever felt you were driving 80 miles an hour with the brakes on? The brakes are either your fear of rejection or a negative self-image. Your expectations create your energy, but you may have inhibitors which block your energy from being channeled effectively.

You need to understand the relationship between your self-image and your expectations. Possessing a negative self-image and low expectations may cause a person to feel comfortable when failing. A positive self-image and high expectations would be a healthy combination. With high expectations, the person would be determined to persevere, while their positive self-image would cause the person to feel worthy of the success they would gain.

To illustrate the dramatic difference between your expectations and your self-image, imagine a person with high expectations, but with a negative self-image. This situation may occur when, in childhood, one parent tells the child, "I expect you to make it on your own, depend on no one and become financially independent," while the other parent says, "You will be a bum the rest of your life. You won't amount to anything."

The first parent creates high expectations. The second parent causes the person to develop a negative self-image. The high expectations create within this person an intense energy to excel, but the negative self-image becomes as a cork on the bottle of their energy. This person probably will take on significant challenges but will be in danger of self-destructing. These people often focus all their energy into one objective such as their work, become a workaholic and run the risk of burnout. They become out of balance and often harm their health, disrupt their relationships with their families and even damage their own mental well-being.

Other examples of the same problem are people who devote all their energy to athletics, such as golf or triathlons, and often lose their families and even their jobs. Balance is the answer. One obsession must enhance the other. Thus, devote part of your day to a strenuous exercise program, your work, your loved ones and solitude. If all your energy becomes focused in just one area, you are vulnerable to burning out or losing the others.

TECHNIQUE 10: TOTAL COMMITMENT

For those of us beginning in selling, we often observe people who are doing quite well financially, seemingly with very little effort. If, however, you were to ask this person to remember how many times a day they were disappointed, multiplied by their years in the business, you might be rather impressed with how much rejection this person has withstood.

If you want to get an airplane off the ground, you need 100 percent throttle. Once you are in the air, you can cruise at 60 percent. Yet certain people beginning in sales are trying to succeed with only a 60-percent effort, and they are "crashing into trees and tumbling into ditches." If you want to succeed, you need to make a Total Commitment and a 100-percent effort. As you succeed, you can begin to cruise and enjoy your financial success without undue stress.

TECHNIQUE 11: TAILORED TECHNIQUE

There are so many ideas and techniques to choose from to succeed. Rather than following the advice of others, you need to develop an approach which is personalized to your unique nature and style—the Tailored technique.

When empowering yourself to function on your own, you need to be creative and develop techniques which are tailored to your personality. For example, if mailing promotional material with an appropriate cover letter before prospecting causes you to feel more comfortable making cold calls, then follow that pattern.

If you have difficulty jogging, then try running with a friend or around a lake so the activity becomes more interesting. Listen to music with a headset or use this time to dialogue with yourself.

Being innovative is a primary factor in managing yourself as part of developing your potential.

TECHNIQUE 12: REWARD

The 12th technique for motivating yourself is Reward. Decide what gift you will give yourself if you achieve your objective. Think of your financial goal. Imagine your goal is $100,000. If you were to earn that income, then what will you give yourself as a reward? Consider a vacation such as seven days in Paris. If you reach your financial expectations, then you deserve that reward.

While high expectations create the determination to persevere, they also can cause certain frustrations, such as demanding perfection.

If you were to reach $80,000, you deserve to give yourself a gift such as a five-day trip to Maui. If you make $60,000, then you may want to consider a three-day weekend in a quiet place, so you can introspect about both your success and how you may do better. If you make $25,000, then how about Newark, in a downtown hotel, for a month. Motivate yourself by deciding on varying levels of gifts for varying levels of success.

TECHNIQUE 13: PUNISHMENT

The 13th technique for disciplining yourself is Punishment. While we prefer to use positive motivation, such as giving ourselves gifts if we succeed, we need to realize that some people do better under pressure.

For example, I have been lecturing internationally for 20 years and I always have been late for airplanes. When the problem occurs on every trip, you begin to realize there must be a reason. After some introspection, I realized that I enjoy being late for airplanes. Being early is boring. When you are early, you know you will make it, and there is no challenge. When you are late, however, the drive becomes exciting, though being overanxious can become absurd.

My new challenge, therefore, is to arrive at the airport early enough to make telephone calls. Then, if I am caught in rush-hour traffic, the danger of missing my flight is minimal. Creating stress as an added energy to increase your anxiousness to succeed can be positive. Avoid overload by knowing when to mellow out rather than becoming irritable.

Decide what you will deny yourself on those days when you have not performed according to your expectations. These techniques become more potent when you merge them together, such as punishment and self-competition. What will you deny yourself if you do not outscore yesterday's performance by at least one point?

Do not deny yourself a strenuous exercise program, time with loved ones, nor solitude, such as meditation, watching a sunset or reading a book. You can deny yourself watching television, playing golf in an electric cart for three hours, drinking caffeine or alcohol or eating dessert. You often have to discipline yourself if you are to stay on target and succeed.

In a market-driven economy, we need to become entrepreneurial and empower ourselves to take on greater responsibility. More specifically, we need to become self-disciplined risk takers and manage ourselves. When you are not on target, you may have to "straighten yourself out."

12

Maximizing Your Performance

Consistency creates self-discipline.

Think of the stress you may have to experience whenever you begin a strenuous exercise program or take on a new challenge at work to improve your financial position. If you ever have difficulty justifying the stress, then read the book by Dr. Victor Frankl, *Man's Search for Meaning*.

During World War II, Dr. Frankl, a psychiatrist, was imprisoned in a concentration camp. Gradually his fellow prisoners realized that there was one freedom they had which could end the suffering of every day—the freedom to die. As these prisoners contemplated this one escape from their suffering, they began to commit suicide. The place was Treblinka and it was filled with sad stories, such as one man convincing his son to kick the chair out from under him so he could hang himself. Dr. Frankl, as a psychiatrist as well as a fellow prisoner, took upon himself the challenge to keep these men alive.

He struggled to think of what he could say to help a man persevere through the pain every day. Finally, he found the answer in a question. The question was so powerful that a man often found the suffering to be more than tolerable, but even meaningful. The question was, "What will you do when you get out?" One man said, "Finish my science project." Another man said, "Finish the book I was writing." Another said, "See my children again."

Suddenly, they understood the relationship between where they were and where they wanted to be, that *if the more you suffer the closer you come to where you want to be, then you can no longer call it suffering but only what you must go through to discover how good you are.* If that single thought could help men in that position, then it also can help you, if you ever have difficulty bridging the gap from where you are to where you want to be.

Breaking Negative Cycles

Your reactions to past experiences create your self-image, which determines your attitudes toward various people and responsibilities. Your attitudes then determine your habits, which eventually determine your results. In turn, your results then justify what you believe to be true, which reinforces your self-image, whether positive or negative.

For example, a negative self-image toward certain responsibilities such as writing proposals or making presentations will cause a negative attitude toward such activities. Avoiding such responsibilities will reduce your effectiveness in your job and often create a negative cycle.

The solution begins with introspection and being honest with yourself. Think of the experiences in your past which might have caused such activities to be beneath your self-image or a threat to your self-image. Then decide where change might occur. You may want to take on a task which would be easy to accomplish to create a positive momentum. Instead you may decide to achieve an objective which is particularly challenging. Then take action by merging those goal-achieving techniques which you feel are most appropriate for your personality.

TECHNIQUE 14: BENEFITS

Think of New Year's Eve and the resolutions you create for yourself, yet too often forget. We may lose interest or become discouraged by the first adversity. Possibly our desire is not great enough to drive us through the disappointment, or maybe the goal was not important enough to be remembered.

The solution is to create the intensity of desire that will enhance our determination to persevere. Consider where this desire comes from, to be willing to suffer through difficult times until we succeed. The origins of our positive energy is in our needs—what we decide we must have if we are to be happy.

Yet if we believe that the objective is not important enough to justify the disappointment we may have to experience to excel, we may then compromise our expectations and forget our aspirations. One solution is to sell ourselves on the Benefits we will gain if we do achieve our objective.

Think of how you persuade a prospect who is interested in your product, but not excited enough to make the investment. You present the benefits as a way of creating enough enthusiasm to gain the buying decision.

You also may need to sell yourself on all the benefits you will gain if you buy into the objectives you are setting for yourself. For example, if your objective is to begin a strenuous exercise program, but you keep losing your determination and therefore your momentum, then list the benefits you will gain if you get in shape:

- I will lose weight and feel good.
- I will eliminate stress and make better decisions.
- I will enjoy the solitude and take time to prioritize my objectives.
- I will create a sense of achievement and a positive momentum.

Then apply the same process to the income you will earn if you fulfill your sales responsibilities:

- I will enjoy the affluence I deserve.
- I will be able to provide more easily for those I care about.
- I will have a sense of achievement which will enhance my self-image and increase my self-esteem.
- I will create new strengths which will allow me to more easily fulfill future obligations.

Sell yourself on how good you will feel after you have reached your objective. Reading the Sunday newspaper is so much more satisfying after you have finished a long bike ride. Otherwise, relaxing can cause you to become bored, restless and depressed.

Watching the evening news can be a pleasant way to relax after a productive day in the business. If, however, you avoided your challenges and were defensive, then the television may remind you of your passive patterns and create guilt. Hopefully, in the future, you will respond positively to justified guilt, sell yourself on all the benefits you will enjoy if you confront the challenges, renew your determination and persevere until you succeed.

TECHNIQUE 15: FEAR

Your fears do not have a face. They are only voices without power. They only have power if you allow them to influence your thinking. Imagine you arrive home, alone, late at night. Your first activity is to turn on the lights. Once you realize that there is no danger, you feel better. You also need to turn the light on your fears and realize that they are empty voices. Attack your fears. Relieve yourself of your fears by telling people what concerns you.

This Fear approach also can help you in prospecting. If a fear is inhibiting you from making calls, then express your fears in your opening line. For example, if you fear that you will disturb the prospect and thus be rejected, then begin the call by saying, "I'm probably catching you at a bad time, so if I am disturbing you, I'll call some other time."

We all have fears. The important factor is how we react to them. While most people allow their fears to demotivate them, some people succeed because of their fears. Possibly their success is based on attacking their fears. The idea that they would allow "faceless voices" to immobilize them is so unacceptable to their positive self-images that they instead do the reverse of what their fears may negatively be suggesting to them.

For example, if their fears were to say, "You can't make your quota." or "You will never reach your objectives of new accounts for the month.", successful people will become even more committed and determined. This is similar to the way some people react against negative influences in their childhood. While most children will become inhibited if they are constantly told, "Watch out, you might hurt yourself." or "You're so stupid, you never will succeed.", some will rebel to such negative feedback. They will prove they can take chances and not get hurt or that they are capable of succeeding.

Think of the negative consequences of not achieving your objectives. For example, if you do not eliminate a negative addiction and develop a positive addiction:

- You frequently will become irritable or moody.
- People will question your maturity.
- You will be less creative and productive.
- You will endanger your health and reduce your energy.
- You will have difficulty respecting yourself.

List all the problems you may experience if you do not reach your financial objectives. Just as you often need to create a sense of urgency when selling a prospect if you are to gain their agreement, so you also need to describe reality to yourself, that change is required. Remind yourself of the seriousness of your situation if you do not succeed.

Recognizing Your Potential

If you appreciate your potential, you will do battle with failure, rather than accept it. Also, when you achieve your objectives, rather than leveling off, you will capitalize on your success. You need to recognize the tremendous potential which exists within you.

For example, a man noticed his car was on fire. He pulled to the side of the road and found the brakes were on fire. He threw water on the brakes; then to make sure the fire was out, he crawled under the car. One of the tires then exploded from the heat. Now the man was pinned under the car and the fire started up again. A 17-year-old man, seeing what was happening and realizing how dangerous the situation was, pulled off to the side of the road. Weighing 140 pounds, he lifted the front of this 3,400-pound car off the man.

The reason why he was able to accomplish this was because he did not think about it. If he had asked himself, "Can I do it?", he would have said, "No way." If he then tried, he would not have succeeded. Instead, he just did it.

You probably are aware of similar stories of people performing phenomenal feats to save someone's life. Maybe you can remember a time when you were successful because you did not think about the difficulty. You just reacted and surprised yourself. Fear is a factor which can illustrate what people can achieve when their negative self-images are not getting in their way.

TECHNIQUE 16: HONESTY

The next technique is Honesty. We need to understand the relationship between our problems and our defense mechanisms. More specifically, our egos may be oversensitive or we may have certain responsibilities which we feel are beneath our self-images, such as paperwork. Often, when we are asked why we are not being productive, our explanations relate to our defense mechanisms rather than the vulnerability which is causing us to protect ourselves.

For example, if you were asked why you have not been closing on certain prospects, you may reply, "I've been procrastinating." Yet procrastination, including laziness and disorganization, are never the problems. They are the protective devices which we use to avoid our problems. We need to be honest with ourselves. More specifically, we may not be closing because we have become dependent on our prospects. They give us hope, that they eventually may buy from us. They also cause us to feel that people like us, which makes us feel good about ourselves.

If we were to ask for a decision and they turned us down, we may feel rejected. We also would lose prospects and therefore lose hope. Better not to close and hope that if we had, they would buy, than close and be rejected and find our optimism was unjustified.

Yet we are reducing our chances of succeeding if we are dishonest with ourselves. If we believe that our problem is being disorganized, then we would assume that the solution is to become organized. We may, however, only be trading one defense mechanism for another. Certain people are very organized. They devote their day to getting ready. They prepare their prospecting calls, study the situation and create their presentation. They spend so much time in preparation that they have little time to take action.

When we recognize the games we play and those fears or apprehensions which really are disturbing us, we may then make significant changes. We hopefully will accept those challenges which, once completed, will create new strengths to replace our vulnerabilities. Then we will have no need to be defensive.

The Subconscious Mind

Another illustration of our potential is dreams. If you are not familiar with the town of Stillwell, Oklahoma, you probably know of

Port Arthur, Texas. Both places are named for Arthur Stillwell. At the age of 16, during the late 1800s, he had a dream that he would meet and marry a woman with a certain name. He knew of no such woman, but four years later, when he was 20, he met and married a woman with that name. He then was working as a clerk for a bank when the dream began again, telling him to build a railroad. He had no money to build a railroad, but he found investors and by the time he was 27, he was a millionaire.

Then the dream began again, this time to build a railroad from the wheat fields of Kansas to the Gulf of Mexico, for in those days there was no railroad going in that direction, so he began construction. Fifty miles before reaching Galveston, the major shipping port on the gulf, his dream returned, telling him to stop building. Even though his investors were upset, for they would receive no return on their investment until the railroad was completed, he followed the voices. Then the dream started again, to continue building, but not to Galveston. Instead, the dream instructed him to go beyond Galveston, into a swampland and construct a new port, which he did, calling it Port Arthur. As soon as the town was constructed, the famous hurricane of the early 1900s hit Texas and totaled Galveston, just missing Port Arthur. One of the reasons why Galveston could rebuild quickly was because Port Arthur was nearby so the material for reconstruction became readily available. Arthur Stillwell then felt comfortable discussing what he had experienced.

TECHNIQUE 17: FORCED SCHEDULING

The next technique for managing yourself is Forced Scheduling. Create, in your day, a schedule that forces you into success patterns. Motivation is very elusive and motivating oneself is intangible. You need to create structure in your life, like the monkey bars in a child's playground. You need handles you can grasp onto, so when you are in trouble, you can pull yourself up.

Develop a schedule each day which forces you into success patterns. Breakfast appointments with prospects and customers can force you out of bed, get you ahead of rush-hour traffic and, by nine o'clock, you already have had a productive morning. Having telephone appointments throughout the day, lunch with an associate to share ideas and prospecting late in the afternoon with your buddy will help you stay on schedule and can assure your success.

Innate Ability

Another factor which demonstrates the tremendous potential within us is illustrated in *Life* magazine's Science Library. In the book entitled *The Mind,* the authors discuss an 11-year-old boy who could play complicated classical music by ear, multiply long numbers at high speed and, if given a date, such as January 2, 1803, could tell you what day of the week it had been. Yet he could not attend school, because he was mentally retarded.

There are three parts of our brain that we need to understand when developing our potential. The first part of our brain contains our innate ability and potential. Unfortunately, some infants experience damage to their brain during childbirth. However, that part of the brain that houses their innate ability is not damaged.

A second part of the brain houses our intelligence, such as our ability to solve problems, be creative and relate to people. If this part is damaged, the child is considered mentally retarded.

The third part of the brain is where our self-image develops. This is the part of the brain which tells us what we can or cannot do, and for some people this area also is damaged. These people have no negative self-images telling them what they cannot do, so their innate ability is expressed spontaneously. The child plays the piano by ear, multiplies long numbers at high speed and possesses a photographic memory.

TECHNIQUE 18: SYMBOLS OF SUCCESS

Buying clothing, a car or a home, which is symbolic of success, can help us feel better about ourselves. We may not yet be as successful as we want to be, but the association with what we have bought can enhance our self-images.

Depending on some materialistic object to improve one's self-image is a superficial way of feeling good about oneself. However, the Symbols of Success technique works. Investing in a home which appreciates and offers tax benefits, as well as eventually paying off the mortgage, can help create financial independence while improving your self-image. When you buy a car that is comfortable and looks good, then each time you drive it, you are symbolically reminding yourself of your own value. When you buy clothes, think of the effect which the suit, dress or tie will have on your self-image.

Never Questioning Oneself

Another factor which can disengage a negative self-image is being mentally unbalanced. Certain people throughout history have been very successful by certain criteria, though they were mentally ill. As an extremely negative example, many years ago, a man was so mentally unbalanced that he almost committed suicide three times. In the end, he actually did.

During a six-month period, he had difficulty taking care of himself and almost starved to death. He could not continue his education because he scored so badly on his exams. His ambitious dreams included taking over the world. He also irritated people and made a nuisance of himself, so he was sent to jail. While behind bars, he wrote a lengthy book explaining how he planned to take over the world.

If you had seen this man in prison, mentally unbalanced and uneducated, you may have had no desire to stop and laugh at him. Yet between 60 and 70 million people had to die before Adolf Hitler was stopped from achieving his goals.

Most people would have heard a voice within their minds telling them, "Adolf, you're a painter, and a poor one at that. You can't take over Germany, Belgium, France, Holland, Estonia, Denmark, Latvia, Norway, Lithuania, Finland, Austria, Czechoslovakia, Poland, Bulgaria, Albania, Rumania, Italy, Egypt and Greece." However, that part of Hitler's mind was not functioning, so he took over 19 nations. Though a negative example, Hitler illustrates what people can accomplish when they have no negative self-images inhibiting them from achieving their objectives.

Ego Confidence

As a last illustration of the phenomenal potential which exists within people, consider ego. Some people possess tremendous egos and, though lacking humility, often are very successful. For example, think of athletes who, in the United States of America, became legends in their own time. Think back to a period between 1968 and 1972 and those athletes with great egos and great success. You would have to mention Joe Namath, Muhammad Ali, Mark Spitz and, if you consider chess a sport, you would include Bobby Fischer.

Remember Joe Namath playing against the Baltimore Colts. His AFL team was considered no match against the senior Baltimore Colts. The night before the game, on national television, Joe Namath did not predict he would win, he guaranteed it; and what he did in that game made him a legend in his own time. Afterward he said, "I was so relaxed, I never felt my arm." When you are convinced that you will succeed, and you have no negative self-image, then you experience no anxiety and success often is spontaneous.

Think about Muhammad Ali in his first major fight against Sonny Liston, the heavyweight champion. The odds were seven to one against Muhammad Ali. The night before the fight, he did not predict he would win, he guaranteed it, because he was going to "float like a butterfly," and he won decisively.

Later, after a forced retirement because of the Vietnam conflict, he fought against George Forman. Without warning his trainers, he decided to experiment. He went up against the ropes and hid his head with his hands and arms. Only his stomach was exposed, and George, one of the strongest boxers in the history of the sport, stood there and worked Ali's gut, round after round, while Ali's trainers pleaded to no avail, "Dance around, keep your distance." In the seventh round, Muhammad Ali peeked out, saw that George was getting tired, hit him once and the fight was over. Think of the confidence a person must have to hang onto the ropes for seven rounds, waiting patiently for his opponent to tire out, and then put him away so quickly. We are discussing ego.

Consider Mark Spitz who, during the 1968 Mexico Olympics, did not do anywhere near as well as he claimed he would. The American public probably was pleased to watch someone lose and perhaps develop humility, than win and become more egotistical. Yet in 1972, Mark Spitz returned, with the same ego confidence he had earlier, and set seven Olympic records. In seven races, he won seven gold medals and set seven world records.

For one last example, if you consider chess a sport, then remember Bobby Fischer in 1972, mailing a telegram to the Chess Federation: "I'm not going. Mail the money to me, for I see no point in making the trip." Bobby Fischer felt it was an insult to have to prove he was the best. Finally, his friends coerced him into making the effort, and what he did against Spasky, based on a scoring device which has been used in chess throughout history, made him the greatest chess player ever. Yet when he returned, his personality had not changed. In fact, Bob Hope interviewed him on television and asked him, "Bobby, I hear there was very little conversation between you and Spasky." Bobby said, "You're right. In the morning, Boris would say 'good morning' to me and at night I would say 'checkmate.' " So, he had not developed much humility.

When you appreciate the tremendous potential within you, then you need to reevaluate the conditioning which creates both your success and your limitations.

The Great Imposter

Assume, for a moment, that you have not really met yourself. Possibly the person you think you are is only a small part of your potential. As long as you believe you know who you are, then you will be consistent in your behavior, though not always for your benefit. If you want to exceed your present performance, you may have to decide that you are capable of more than you realize.

You probably are familiar with Ferdinand Walpo Dimera, though you may know him as "The Great Imposter." Tony Curtis played the role in the movie. Dimera was once a surgeon, a priest and a professor of psychology in a university, with no background or qualifications in any of these occupations.

During the 1920s, Ferdinand's father was wealthy. They owned two movie theaters and a mansion and had a maid, and Ferdinand attended a private school. Then, during the depression, they lost their business, the house, the maid and the private school and moved to a poor neighborhood.

Ferdinand would ask his father, "Will we ever go back to the house?", for the house symbolized the identity of someone of importance. They never returned to that house, however, and for the rest of his life Dimera tried to discover who he was. Having lost his image of himself as a successful person, and refusing to accept himself as a failure, he continuously challenged himself to discover his identity, to discover what he was capable of achieving.

Do not assume that you know who you are. Rather wonder what your real potential may be. Then challenge yourself to break through your present limitations and expand your sense of identity. Think of how, if you had been born into a different environment with a different childhood, you might possess a different self-image. Who, then, would you really be?

TECHNIQUE 19: ACTING AS IF...

The next technique to improve your self-image is "Acting As If...." If all the suggestions and techniques you have been given have failed you, then maybe you do not see yourself as the person you need to be. The solution: Just fake it. Play the role.

Many people are offended at the thought of "acting as if" or faking it. However, are you the same person today that you were when you were 12 or 13? You probably have matured since then. Remember how you developed these qualities?

Initially you felt inadequate, such as when telling jokes, speaking in front of a group or expressing your feelings. Then you watched someone who had what you needed. Possibly, this person was a visiting uncle or aunt, an actor on stage or an actress in the movies. Then you thought to yourself, 'If I were as humorous as this person, I may have more fun.' or 'If I were more confident, people may respect me more.' So you started playing the role. You began acting as if you were this person. As people responded positively, you started thinking, 'Maybe this is me.' Gradually you integrated the quality into your personality. Now, as the years pass, you may have forgotten where this attribute came from.

For example, a man probably can think back to when he was 13 or 14 and the first time he called a girl on the telephone and asked for a date. Imagine how he would have sounded if he projected the way he actually felt. "Hi, this is, uh, this is, Art Mortell. And you know the junior, whatever this dance is called. Well, I was wondering if by chance you may want to consider the thought that you may like the idea of at least thinking about being interested in the possibility of...my mother told me to call you and ask if you...you wouldn't want to go with me, would you?"

If he projected the way he actually felt, he may have spoken this way. So instead he said, "Hi, this is Art Mortell. You know the junior prom this Saturday night? I know you will enjoy yourself with me. What time should I pick you up? Would you prefer seven or seven-thirty?" She said, "You're pretty cool, aren't you?", and he said, "Yes, I sure am." Suddenly, he felt confident in himself.

If all else fails, play the role until you become the person you want to be.

Describe the qualities of the ideal salesperson and the characteristics of the image they project. Next, decide what qualities you need to develop within your own self, or at least in the way you project to others. Then begin playing the role until these desired characteristics seem natural.

Another example of merging these techniques to better assure your success is to use "Acting as if..." with Acceptance Span. Do not make such a radical change in your personality that if you gain positive feedback, you feel that you did not succeed, because the qualities you were projecting were not really an extension of your true self. Otherwise, you may feel that you are an imposter, and your success will not translate into self-esteem. When the changes are gradual rather than exaggerated, the positive feedback will be more believable, and you will be able to more easily integrate the quality into your self-image.

TECHNIQUE 20: EXAGGERATION

The next technique to consider is Exaggeration. One reason people have difficulty making a total commitment is because if they fail, they fail totally. For this reason, when they try, they try only to a small extent. Then, if they fail, they fail only in a small way.

While there are circumstances in which cautiousness is appropriate, we often need to be ambitious and make a total commitment. Think of a way in which you can "go both barrels" while still protecting yourself from disappointment and embarrassment.

For example, you decide to capitalize on your:

- Warm, sensitive nature by being aggressive;
- Quiet, introspective style by being emotional and enthusiastic;
- Aggressive, confident personality by being friendly and gentle; and
- Expressive, humorous style by being serious and introspective.

Exaggerate the qualities which you want to develop. Practice in front of a mirror. Ask a friend to videotape your role-playing effort. When you exaggerate without anyone observing who will be critical or judgmental, you get to feel the qualities that you want to develop. Then, when you use the quality without exaggeration, the process will feel natural.

You also can exaggerate within the actual activities. For example, if you are experiencing difficulty prospecting, then devote one day to marathon cold calling. Begin early, prospect through rush hour and take only a few minutes for lunch; then determine how many cold calls you can make in one day. Afterward, your normal objective, such as 40 cold-call conversations, may feel more comfortable.

Many of these goal-achieving techniques may seem contradictions of each other. Yet people are different, and an approach which motivates one person may demotivate someone else. Determine, within your own creativity, the combination of techniques which might be most appropriate for your personality.

Disengaging Your Self-Image

Hypnosis is another factor which demonstrates our innate potential when we have no limitations. You probably are familiar with hypnosis being used to stop pain in childbirth, surgery and dentistry. The hypnotist says to the person, "You are a leaf, floating effortlessly, floating downward, becoming relaxed and letting yourself go." The person becomes so relaxed that he or she does not question what is being suggested. Then the hypnotist says, "There is no pain," and the patient feels no pain. Just as people can lift the front of a car, merely by disengaging their own negative self-images, so can hypnosis illustrate what people can accomplish when they do not question themselves.

TECHNIQUE 21: GOYA

Before presenting this technique for assuring your success, first consider why other techniques may not have helped you. Whenever you want to succeed in achieving a specific goal, the first step is to think. Specifically, to think of what you want to do. When you think of what you want to do, unfortunately, certain doubts may come to mind, for instance, that you possibly may fail.

Thinking of failure can cause you to become depressed, which may motivate you to procrastinate. By avoiding your responsibilities, your doubts will begin to convert into negative convictions, that you never should have tried in the first place, creating a negative desire to quit.

Realize that this negative cycle began with thinking.

If all else fails, stop thinking and use the GOYA technique, which is Getting Off Your Seat. Stop thinking and just do it. Once you have made the effort, then evaluate your results. Regardless of what has happened, you will not have failed. Within part of what you have accomplished will be some success, and the other part will indicate where you need to become more creative and try a different approach. Remember, you cannot fail. You are merely determining those areas in which you need to become more effective. Adversity is an arena for creativity.

The next illustration reminds us of the value of not thinking but just doing it. During the depression, a 13-year-old boy's family could not afford to send him to school so he sold shoelaces on a street corner. He saved his money and when he was in his 20s, he opened a small retail store. In his 30s, he opened a department store; in his 40s, he built stores nationally; and in his 50s, he was a multimillionaire.

One day a man asked him, "Here you are with all this fantastic wealth and yet no educational background. What do you attribute your success to?"

He said, "It's very simple. I buy a product for one dollar, I sell it for two dollars and I'm happy with one percent."

Sometimes we think too much of all the reasons why we may not succeed. Often we need to stop thinking and just do it. Just stop smoking. Start dieting. Do it! Begin an exercise program. Make those prospecting calls. Express yourself to someone, regardless of feeling inhibited. Confront the conflict and deal with the confrontation. Just do it! Later on, you can think of how you can do better.

The greatest form of stress often is not in the experience which causes it, but in thought of the experience. Think of those occasions when your noble intention was to exercise the next morning. Then, when you awoke, just the thought of running or cycling was stressful. The bed seemed so warm and comfortable, and the idea of physical exertion, particularly if the morning was cold and dark, turned you off. Many people, when they feel like exercising, lie down until the feeling goes away.

Yet if you were to just do it, you soon would feel exhilarated. You would eliminate stress, prioritize your objectives, develop creative thoughts, enjoy the solitude, feel a sense of achievement and often make your best decisions. The challenge is not so much in the challenge, but in confronting and getting started. Once in motion, the process often is effortless and even stimulating.

Some people cannot run a mile or even a quarter of a mile. Yet these same people, if they were to accept the physical discomfort and persevere, soon would discover that stress can make them more resilient. As the distance of each Saturday morning run is extended, the aspirations begin to transform into endurance. Soon the fat becomes muscle, the cardiovascular system is in shape and a 26-mile marathon is completed.

Selling follows the same pattern. The emotional discomfort causes your ego to become more resilient. Soon making the prospecting calls, which may have been difficult, becomes an effortless process.

TECHNIQUE 22: VIVID IMAGINATION

The last technique for improving your self-image is entitled Vivid Imagination. While this is one of the most traditional and effective techniques for developing one's potential, it also is very elusive. This technique is based on the idea that your subconscious mind cannot tell the difference between a real or an imagined thought. Your subconscious only follows what you consciously believe to be true, whether real or imagined.

If this idea seems strange to you, then think back to the 1968 Mexico City Olympics. Dick Fosbury was about to attempt the high jump. The bar was set at seven feet, four and a fraction inches. Fosbury's technique today is considered quite orthodox, but, in 1968, when he created this approach, it was regarded as extremely unusual. When he reached the bar, he would turn and jump backwards. On that Sunday afternoon, he had to jump a foot and a half over the top of his head, backwards, with the lowest part of his body never as low as that bar. Those who watched him on that Sunday afternoon, with his fists clenched, rocking back and forth, wondered if he would even try.

He explained afterward, "I couldn't psyche myself into it, nor could I imagine myself succeeding. There were too many distractions in my mind. I knew that around the world by satellite millions of people were watching me. If I were to succeed, I would set a new Olympic record. I had to jump a foot and a half over the top of my head, backwards, the lowest part of my body never as low as that bar. There was so much pressure on me that I couldn't get myself into it. All I was trying to do was clear my mind of all these distractions."

Fists clenched, he rocked back and forth, as though staring at a candle in hypnosis or repeating a mantra in meditation, until finally his mind went blank.

As he explained, "Now I could see myself running perfectly, picturing myself turning backwards, leaping into the air, visualizing myself a foot and a half over the top of my head, feeling myself land safely and hearing the roar of the crowd. At the moment that I could see myself succeeding, the easy part was physical."

On his first try, he jumped a foot and a half over the top of his head, backwards, the lowest part of his body never within two inches of the bar. He never did it again, but at that one moment when he stood on the edge of fulfilling his greatest dream, he was able to so vividly imagine himself succeeding that the easy part was physical.

You probably have heard of people who walk barefoot on hot coals, the temperature measured at 600 degrees. If you drop a piece of paper, it will burst into flames before reaching the coals. When these people finish walking barefoot on these hot coals, they brush the ashes off the bottoms of their feet, and there is no negative reaction.

This accomplishment is a two-step process. The first step is tabula rasa, which translates into blank slate or clear mind. The second step is the visualization process in which the person imagines that he or she is walking on wet, cool rocks. This visualization was the same technique that Fosbury had used.

Perhaps a greater accomplishment in Mexico City in 1968 was that of Bob Beamon, an American long jumper. The world record going into the 1968 Mexico Olympics for the long jump was 27 feet, 4 and a fraction inches. If you want to appreciate how far one must travel before landing 27 feet away, take a moment to measure the distance.

On that Sunday afternoon, Bob Beamon leaned forward and stared into the distance. Afterward, his explanation was similar to Dick Fosbury's, "I was trying to disengage from all the pressure of the present and see myself in the future. Suddenly, it was as though I was watching a movie of myself. I could see myself running step by step, with the perfect stride, hit the wood at the right point and make a perfect leap."

World records usually are broken by a fraction of an inch or a fraction of a second. On that Sunday afternoon, however, Bob Beamon became so psyched, which means so vividly seeing himself succeed before he tried, that his subconscious mind had no choice but to fulfill the imagery.

On that Sunday afternoon, he went through 27 feet, he went through 28 feet and he did not come down until he reached 29 feet 2 inches. He shattered the world's record by two full feet.

When he landed, he threw himself to the side so he would not fall back and lose what he had gained. When he looked back to see what he had accomplished, he collapsed, his head in his hands, and he cried. He had gone beyond his own expectations.

Many of us make a very serious effort in our lives to achieve our expectations. If we can capitalize on failure and rejection and eliminate any negative self-images, we can succeed. Sometimes, though rarely, people so vividly imagine themselves succeeding that they exceed their own expectations. Therefore, before prospecting, making a presentation or closing, visualize yourself as the person you need to be. Through imagery, you can see yourself succeeding as you prepare your mind to achieve your objectives.

Develop the duality of your own personality. See yourself as someone else. One person is the actor, performing on the stage of life, and the other is the director, who objectively and brilliantly guides the actor through the process.

Imagine the people who are listening to your presentation. As you begin speaking, your director *monitors* your effectiveness, such as your speaking style, your expressions and your choice of words. This objective person then interrupts you whenever you seem off target and offers suggestions to *modify* your approach.

Whenever your director interrupts you, the audience which you are visualizing in front of you is very patient. These people allow you to begin again until you are proficient with that segment of your presentation. Then you move on to the next part. Later, when you actually make the prospecting calls or presentation, you will sense the strange satisfaction of knowing how good you already are and how much these people already accept you.

MULTIPLYING TALENTS

In review, decide which combination of these goal-achieving techniques you can use to remain disciplined until you achieve your objectives. You need to select those words which can help you manage yourself until you succeed.

As an illustration of words which can motivate us and what words can turn us off, a minister had a horse which was not very smart. Yet if the minister said, "Praise the Lord," the horse would start. If he said, "Hallelujah," the horse would gallop, and if he said, "Amen," the horse would stop. One day a man needed a horse and the minister offered him his, explaining that while the horse was not intelligent, it would follow instructions. "If you say 'Praise the Lord,' the horse will start, if you say 'Hallelujah,' the horse will gallop, and if you say 'Amen,' the horse will stop."

The man got on the horse, said "Praise the Lord" and off he went. He said "Hallelujah" and was galloping along when he saw in the distance a cliff, so he said to the horse, "Whoa, whoa," but the horse kept galloping. He said "Whoa, whoa" and the horse continued galloping when, almost at the edge of the cliff, the man recalled the word and yelled "Amen" and the horse stopped right at the edge of the cliff. "Well," he said, "Praise the Lord."

The words which turn one person on may turn off someone else. Select those techniques which can help you develop your potential. Understand the value of stress and maximize your performance.

13

Achieving Your Objectives

We have within us all the talents we need to help ourselves. All we need, to lift ourselves up, is to multiply our talents.

Remember the story of the man and the horse. As you can imagine, he went off the cliff. About a third of the way down, and the bottom still a thousand feet below, he caught a branch and, hanging on, began to pray for the first time in many years, "O Lord, help me," and a voice thundered down, "My son, what is the problem?" and he called back, "O Lord, I am hanging from a branch. Please save me." The Voice responded, "My son, do you believe in me?" and he said, "Yes, Lord, I believe in you." Then the Voice said, "My son, if you believe in me, then let go of the branch." And the man called back, "Is there anyone else up there who can help me?"

Review the techniques presented in the previous pages which can help you develop your potential and achieve your objectives. First decide what you want to achieve, such as acquiring 100 new customers during the next 12 months or a specific income. Then select those techniques which, when combined, will help you discipline yourself to stay on target.

TECHNIQUE 1: POSITIVE AFFIRMATIONS

Convert your goal into a positive affirmation, such as, "I am a $100,000-a-year producer." Remember that your subconscious does not respond to words such as think, maybe, hope, going to, will, would or possibly. Your subconscious mind only follows what you believe to be true and in the present tense.

Keep your positive affirmation visible, such as on your desk. The constant reminder, "I am worthy of financial independence" or "Rejection turns me on," soon may become part of your self-image. In no time, the challenge will become effortless and without stress.

TECHNIQUE 2: DESCRIPTIVE TECHNIQUE

Describe the perfect person for your job: the way they would think when experiencing adversity, their reactions toward people who were negative toward them, how they would deal with stress, the ways they would keep themselves disciplined, how they would feel about themselves and the images they would project.

Then decide where change may occur, such as the way you react to hostile people or the style of personality which you project.

Imagine that you are the director of a Broadway play and you are explaining to a person who is auditioning for the part: "This is what motivates you, these are your feelings, this is the person you are and the way you project." The person auditioning says, "I am not the kind of person to project such qualities." You would say, "Excuse me, but I was not asking you to be yourself, but rather to play the role."

Describe the person you need to be if you are to succeed and then manage yourself through that process.

TECHNIQUE 3: ACCEPTANCE SPAN

Never compromise your expectations of achieving those objectives which fulfill your potential. Otherwise, you will compromise your self-esteem.

If you are experiencing difficulty achieving your expectations, you may have to reevaluate what you will need to do each day if you are to succeed.

Set goals which stimulate you without overwhelming yourself. For example, you may have two dozen projects in a day. If you think of how much you need to accomplish, you may experience so much stress as to not even begin. Decide how many projects you can be thinking of at one time without the danger of short-circuiting. Possibly, the number of activities is three. Select your first challenge, while the other two create a sense of purpose which stimulates you into a positive momentum of anticipation. Then, as you complete one project, add another.

Whether in increasing your prospecting calls each day or improving the image you are projecting, your success may occur more easily if you break down your challenge into incremental steps.

TECHNIQUE 4: COMMITMENT TO OTHERS

A lack of self-discipline often occurs when we think of confronting certain difficult challenges. Life may become defensive if we have no one forcing us to take the initiative and persevere. Yet in our childhood, we often succeeded, whether in school, playing the piano or learning how to swim, because someone forced us into making the effort.

You can re-create the same process by committing yourself to people who you would not want to disappoint. You may not enjoy having people expecting you to succeed. You can manage yourself more efficiently, however, if you tell people what you plan to achieve. Obligate yourself to those who are interested in your progress and allow the commitment to manage you into consistency and success.

TECHNIQUE 5: COMPETITION

Consider competing with someone who has those qualities you emulate. The contest may be based on reaching a particular objective for a month, such as income. Even if your competitor wins the contest by gaining better results, you also may have won. For example, the challenge may have increased your income. Also, competing with someone you emulate may help you develop qualities that you need.

The competition also can be based on activity rather than on results. More specifically, decide what activity is your weak link. Possibly your difficulty is in prospecting or gaining appointments. Then compete with someone within the activity. For example, how many total calls were made, how many contacts were established and how many prospects were developed. Competition can stimulate you to stay on target.

TECHNIQUE 6: EMULATION

Decide where you may need to make certain changes, such as in the way you think when you fail or how you react to people who are hostile toward you. Next, determine which person you know who is successful because of their philosophy of life or the way they deal with confrontation.

Then practice thinking the same way as this person. For example, you may ask the person what their thoughts might be when experiencing difficulty. Then begin repeating these thoughts in your mind, as through a hypnotic suggestion, such as "Rejection turns me on."

If you need to become more effective when dealing with hostile people, then practice the techniques which they use, such as, "I'm sorry I have insulted you. However, I would not be so persistent if it were not for the fact that you are a very successful person. I really would appreciate if I could at least take you to lunch so you could give me your opinions of what I am trying to sell."

Once you have adopted their thinking or behavioral process, you then can adapt it to your existing personality.

TECHNIQUE 7: LEADERSHIP

Invite someone to join you in your next project, such as jogging, prospecting or taking a personal-development program. If the person agrees to go with you, such as when contacting prospects for appointments, then you may have no choice but to begin. Demonstrating how to achieve an objective automatically creates the initiative. Showing someone else how to succeed can create the momentum which you need.

TECHNIQUE 8: BUDDY SYSTEM

Take your major challenge, such as making your quota or reaching your financial objectives, and decide what activity requires your primary attention, such as prospecting. Then ask a friend to join you. This is not the same as Leadership in which you help someone else. Rather, the purpose of a buddy system is sharing.

If you are both making presentations, then work on the same project together. Understand the concept of synergism, in which two people together can create more ideas and gain better results than the total of their efforts if they were working separately. A numerical illustration of this process is one plus one equals three.

Completing your presentation then brings you to the next stage—a rehearsal in which you offer suggestions to each other. Then your buddy joins you on your presentation, and you are supportive when your buddy meets with their prospect.

Some salespeople are very effective in team selling, in which they balance each other's strengths. For example, one person might be particularly knowledgeable about the technical details of the product, while their buddy might be charming and persuasive when making the presentation. Such a buddy system could assure their success, while alone they may be less effective, experience difficulty or even fail.

Another value in synergistic selling is when two salespeople play the "good guy, bad guy" role. The more aggressive salesperson makes the call. If their decisive style gains the respect of the dominant prospect or causes a subservient person to feel secure, then the sale may easily follow. If the assertive salesperson begins to antagonize the prospect, however, the "good guy" contacts the prospect, apologizes for their buddy, asks what problems exist and presents the product in a conversational style.

Decide in which responsibility you need to become more effective, ask a friend to join you and share the challenge.

TECHNIQUE 9: SELF-COMPETITION

If you compare yourself with people who have attained greater success than you, you may feel inadequate and frustrated, which can cause you to be less effective. If you compare yourself with people who are not doing as well as you, then you may feel comfortable when you fail. Instead, you need to compare yourself with the person you were yesterday and extend yourself beyond your past performance.

Decide how much failure you can tolerate before you want to stop trying. If you can handle a little more than yesterday, you are developing momentum. If you are experiencing difficulty dealing with rejection, then play a numbers game and give yourself points for every effort. Then outscore yesterday's efforts. Competing with yourself can assure your continuous success.

TECHNIQUE 10: TOTAL COMMITMENT

Ask yourself why people often have difficulty making a total commitment. Possibly for fear of failure, for if we make a total commitment and we fail, we fail totally. For this reason, many people will make a partial effort to succeed, for if they fail, they will feel only partially upset.

Yet achieving the primary objectives of life, such as your physical well-being, your financial well-being, your relationship with loved ones and your emotional well-being, requires a total commitment.

TECHNIQUE 11: TAILORED TECHNIQUE

Remember that adversity is an arena for creativity. Allow failure to stimulate your thinking and innovate. Allow rejection to motivate you to develop new techniques which are tailored to your personality and the challenges you confront.

If your primary concern is prospecting throughout the day, for example, then create an approach which can help you make as many contacts as possible. First decide what techniques you can use which will be productive and results-oriented. Then think of how to modify your approach so that you do not experience too much rejection. In other words, you want to feel comfortable.

One approach is to separate your prospecting into such activities as cold calling, following up with people who have expressed interest, calling existing clients for referrals and speaking with the support people of prospects who are unavailable to gather information. Then consider how vulnerable or resilient you feel. In other words, in those moments when you are feeling confident, contact qualified prospects who have been hostile. If you are becoming worn down by negative feedback, then make cold calls using a gentle technique such as, "I'm not trying to sell you, for the odds are that you do not need me at this time. I just wanted you to know I'm available, and I would enjoy working with you. Is there a time in the future when it would be appropriate to give you a call?" Be imaginative and develop techniques that are tailored to your personality.

TECHNIQUE 12: REWARD

When I was a child, I would discipline myself to study by rewarding myself with television. If I completed a certain percentage of my school work, then I would watch television for a given time period.

Merge Reward with the Acceptance Span Technique and give yourself incremental gifts for incremental levels of achievement. For example, if you make 50 cold-call contacts in a given day, then decide what reward you will give yourself. Possibly you have earned dinner and a movie.

Try merging Reward with Vivid Imagination and have a picture of the present you will give yourself if you achieve your objective. Possibly, you can keep a picture of your gift on your desk, as a constant reminder of what you will reward yourself if you succeed. This continual reminder of where you want to be in the future can help you make sacrifices today.

For example, if your reward is a vacation to Tahiti, then place a photograph of the islands on your desk or bathroom mirror. The visual reminder of your gift can assure your determination to reach your financial goal.

TECHNIQUE 13: PUNISHMENT

Children often are motivated by the thought of denial: "If you don't clean up your room, you cannot go out and play." While this may cause a child to rebel when they are older, and "trash" their room when they are an adult, your situation today might be very different.

You may know what you want, such as succeeding in your present business challenge and gaining financial independence. Yet an obstacle may appear in your path. Remove the barrier by disciplining yourself through the activity which is blocking you.

Decide at this time what you will take away from yourself or sacrifice if you do not achieve our objective for the day. Then, if you begin to procrastinate, the punishment which you have planned, such as no golf for the weekend, may cause enough stress to force you to persevere. This technique can be combined with Commitment to Others, such as telling your spouse or manager what you will deny yourself if you do not reach your activity level for the day or week.

TECHNIQUE 14: BENEFITS

The technique of Reward can be enhanced if you sell yourself on all the benefits you will gain if you achieve the objective.

For example, if you are experiencing difficulty prospecting consistently, then sell yourself on all the benefits you will gain if you persevere, such as:

- I will develop so many clients that I no longer will need to prospect, but instead will enjoy repeat business and referral selling.
- I will reach my financial objectives and be able to enjoy traveling.
- I can build the house I always have dreamed of.

Strengthen these benefits by converting them into positive affirmations:

- I have so many clients that I only have time to enjoy repeat business and referral selling.
- I am doing so well financially that I can afford to travel to all the places that I always have imagined.
- I am living in the house which once was only a dream.

The more you believe you already have gained these benefits, the less you will accept your present position and the more motivated you will be to stay active until you have created the desired results.

TECHNIQUE 15: FEAR

Think of all the negative consequences if you do not achieve your financial objectives. Be specific and focus on that part of your work which you tend to neglect, such as contacting your most qualified decision maker. Then list all the problems you will experience if you do not make the calls and therefore never reach your financial goals, such as:

- I always will be struggling to pay my bills.
- I will be critical of myself for not being able to afford what I want.
- My associates and family will not think positively of me.

Decide what you need to do, within the way you think, which will motivate you to confront your own apprehensions. You will feel better if you can get through those challenges which frustrate you. You want the storm behind you.

TECHNIQUE 16: HONESTY

There are two great words: *Know thyself.* If we do not understand ourselves, particularly regarding the relationship between the vulnerabilities of our egos and the defense mechanisms we have developed to protect our egos, then we may be destined to repeat our self-defeating patterns.

For example, warmth and sensitivity might be your primary strengths. If your way of protecting your ego from rejection is to become warmer and more sensitive, then you may succeed in disarming people and not being rejected. Yet your overcompensation of friendliness may block your potential aggressiveness, preventing you from being productive and achieving your goals.

Be honest with yourself.

The more aware you are of why you are avoiding important responsibilities, the more likely you may decide, "I am allowing childish defensiveness to get in the way of my own objectives. I refuse to continue in such absurdity. I will drop my protective devices and attack my fears."

TECHNIQUE 17: FORCED SCHEDULING

Create a schedule in your day which forces you to succeed. For example:

7:00 A.M. Breakfast meeting with your buddy.

8:00 A.M. Appointment with a prospect.

9:00 A.M. A planned meeting with a secretary to review proposals.

9:30 A.M. Fulfilling a promise you made to your manager that you would complete 15 contacts by lunch.

12:30 P.M. Appointment with a customer for lunch as an expression of appreciation and to explore additional applications.

2:00 P.M. Appointment with a prospect to make a presentation.

3:30 P.M. Prospecting with your buddy on the telephone competitively or face-to-face as a way of sharing the challenge and critiquing each other's performance.

5:00 P.M. Appointment with a prospect who agreed to avoid rush hour, so you can review their requirements and offer a few possible solutions.

6:00 P.M. Paperwork and organizing the next day's schedule.

Think of how often you have traveled home at the end of a day and have been disturbed to realize how little you had accomplished. Without a plan of action, you often may feel lethargic, begin to procrastinate and receive nominal results. You have to be honest and admit that you were just "going through the motions." Develop a schedule which manages you throughout the day and creates productive activity and satisfying results.

TECHNIQUE 18: SYMBOLS OF SUCCESS

Decide what clothing, such as the tie a man may wear or the jewelry a woman may wear, which will remind you of the person you are and deserve to be.

Unfortunately, many people are so unsure of themselves that they depend on lucky charms or an expensive car for a sense of their own strengths or success.

Use this technique, not to compensate for your own potential and ability, but to encourage you to extend yourself and multiply your talents.

Whenever I have extended myself financially, such as building a home which fulfilled one of my dreams and improved my long-term investment position, my own self-image has been enhanced and my income has increased.

Take a step into the future, of acquiring what you deserve, such as a more valuable home or clothing which reminds you of your own importance, and let these symbols motivate you to perform those activities which convert your dreams into reality.

TECHNIQUE 19: ACTING AS IF...

Decide how you want to feel, such as confident. Then project the kind of personality that people depend on as an authority. If you convince people you are an authority and they accept you as such, then the positive feedback will justify the image you are projecting and you will feel confident.

If you want to feel excited, but you feel apprehensive, then speak with enthusiasm. If your energy is fine-tuned to the other person's style, then you may gain the reactions you desire. Their positive feedback will soon cause you to feel the way you want to feel—enthusiastic.

All the characteristics of all the people you have ever observed are within the spectrum of your potential. You can develop any one of them by merely playing the role. In other words, if you want people to like you, then project the quality of friendliness which is appropriate. If you are accepting of other people and relate to their needs, then you are increasing the chances of their acceptance of you.

Take the initiative in the relationship and play the role until you gain the response which causes you to feel the way you want to feel. Then the projection of the desired quality becomes a natural reaction.

TECHNIQUE 20: EXAGGERATION

People who go cold turkey on smoking often never smoke again.

People who fast for a day discover that they do not die.

People who exaggerate what they are trying to accomplish often discover that "if you aim for the stars you at least may reach the moon."

If you are having difficulty making 20 cold calls in a day, then make 100. The next day you may easily make 30.

Consider taking an acting class. All salespeople, as well as managers, should practice "acting as if..." with the opportunity to exaggerate the qualities which they want to develop. Gradually, the qualities become natural and we become more than we have been before.

TECHNIQUE 21: GOYA

Thinking > of how to do it > causes doubts > that we may fail > generating anxiety > creating depression > causing ineffectiveness > and negative results > which convert our doubts into negative convictions > which negatively motivate us > to quit.

If your thinking process causes this type of negative chain reaction, then stop thinking and just take action.

Once you "throw yourself in the pool of water," you soon will be refreshed and stimulated. When you throw yourself into your business, such as when you are prospecting, you soon may be enthusiastic and have positive momentum.

Just do it.

Rather than saying, "I can't do it," you have made the effort and now can ask yourself, "How can I do it better?"

TECHNIQUE 22: VIVID IMAGINATION

If your objective is to overcome your fear of failure, then, whenever you attempt to succeed within a challenge in which you are apprehensive, imagine yourself succeeding before you try.

Also imagine yourself persevering whenever you experience disappointment. Before a game of tennis or a presentation, visualize yourself as the person you need to be.

Imagine yourself succeeding before you try and you may feel more comfortable when confronting the challenge. The more you visualize yourself as being successful, the more confident you may become, and soon you may feel comfortable. By changing your self-image, you can change your results.

If visualizing yourself succeeding does not help, then imagine why you are experiencing difficulty seeing yourself as the person you want to be. For example, if you have a fear of being embarrassed, and therefore tend to be inhibited, imagine yourself as being spontaneous. See yourself acting foolishly. Understand that the possibility of humiliation is not as serious as never achieving your objectives. Then imagine yourself reacting confidently when people are being amused with your difficulty. Convert the humiliation into humor until the embarrassing situation is working for your benefit.

Think of the length of your life and how many times you have repeated the same thinking and behavior. You have spent many years becoming the person you are today. While these techniques can assure your success, you also may need to be innovative in the way you use them and be willing to persevere until you are proficient.

A few days or a few weeks might be needed before your image of yourself, your attitudes and your behavior begins to change, and thus your results. If you merge these techniques into a combination that is personalized to your unique nature, you can accelerate the process.

THE CHALLENGE TO CHANGE

There is a map of the history of the world which visually illustrates the rise and fall of 21 civilizations. The map graphically shows Egypt expanding and engulfing almost the entire map of Western civilization. Then Egypt was gone, replaced by Greece, which rose and fell, to be replaced by Rome, which also went through the same process. This map so intrigued me that I began taking graduate courses in history at California State College in Los Angeles to discover if there was any single factor that caused this dramatic rise and fall of so many great civilizations.

The first country to begin exploration was Portugal. In the year 1215, the Portuguese gained their independence from the Moors, and filled with an adventuresome spirit, they built larger ships and explored along the coast of Africa, on to India, and returned to Lisbon with a 60 percent return on their investment.

The great wealth of the Portuguese became a challenge to England, France, Spain and the Netherlands, who began competing with Portugal. Magellan was the captain of a Portuguese ship which was the first to travel around the world, though he did not survive the trip. The Portuguese colonized a major part of the earth, with Brazil alone many times larger than Portugal. Then, suddenly, their empire was lost, their wealth was gone and they returned to the past. The reason: The children of the Portuguese were inheriting the wealth, but they were not inheriting the challenge. At that point, their success collapsed.

In another example, consider Rome. In the beginning, the Roman citizen was called to battle and Rome grew rapidly. Each city-state joined to accept the challenge of expanding their civilization. The wealth of the empire, however, caused future generations to desire only bread and circus and the empire collapsed internally. In each civilization, you will find the same pattern. As long as the people were challenged, their accomplishment was significant. Once the wealth was inherited, but not the challenge, the nation would collapse internally.

You have heard the statement that "Nothing succeeds like success." This is not true, for too often success causes a satisfaction which culminates in apathy. We lose our desire to grow and achieve and soon we fail. This pattern can apply to a sports team, a country, a company or an individual.

It may almost be better to say, "Nothing succeeds like failure," for some people allow failure to disturb them until they are stimulated to change and become more effective. Too often, however, failure causes people to become discouraged, depressed and defensive. The only true thought is that "Nothing succeeds like a challenge." Decide in what way you will challenge yourself to grow, achieve and gain self-esteem.

Index